DREAM IT
CHOOSE IT
LIVE IT

The PROVEN SYSTEM
to Create Your Dream
Entrepreneur Lifestyle

DAN WARBURTON

Dream It Choose It Live It

First published in 2020 by

Panoma Press Ltd
48 St Vincent Drive, St Albans, Herts, AL1 5SJ, UK
info@panomapress.com
www.panomapress.com

Book layout by Neil Coe.

978-1-784529-16-1

The right of Dan Warburton to be identified as the author of this work has been asserted in accordance with sections 77 and 78 of the Copyright, Designs and Patents Act 1988.

A CIP catalogue record for this book is available from the British Library.

This book is available online and in bookstores.

Real Words About Dream It Choose It Live It

"Just finished reading this gift of a book. It's inspiring, compassionate and a lot better than many of my favourites, and I've read a lot. The method is clearly explained and reminded me of how powerful the session was when you took me through it, your energy is infectious and this comes across in the book too, great work. Great work."

Rod Milicevic, CEO at Glass Aftercare

"Dan, massive thanks for changing my life. I highly recommend Dan's book. Me and my other half could read this book over and over again!"

Alexandra Natalia, Committed Entrepreneur

"Hey Dan I'm reading your book and enjoying it a lot."

Alex Garcez, Published Speed Reading Expert and Flow State Consultant

"I warmly recommend this book, many insights for entrepreneurs."

San Inyoman, Business Coach

"Great book Dan, thank you for these very interesting and powerful words. Once I started reading it I couldn't stop. It's definitely given me knowledge in how to start living my dreams and not just dream about them. Well done Dan."

Monica Gergely, Director and Executive Producer at J-Blockbuster Films

"Reading your book Dan, I'm really enjoying it."

Sara Pankhurst, Entrepreneur

"I grabbed my copy and I am loving it already."

Charity Nyoike, Investment Consultant

"I have just read Dan's book and it's a great read filled with his own story of transformation and accounts of those who he has helped. More than this though it contains practical steps to transforming negative beliefs into new possibilities. The positivity and power of this book is going to help many people reach and attain their greatness. The first step on the pathway to ultimate success for some may be reading this extraordinary book."

Tim Williams, Spiritual Guide, Philanthropist and Thought Leader

"Wow Dan, I just finished your book online and I loved it. It's just perfect. So amazing and inspiring."

Minati Nag, International Speaker and Entrepreneur

Contents

Dream It Choose It Live It
At A Glance

Dream It Choose It Live It is a practical guide to mindset transformation for ambitious, time-poor or struggling professionals and entrepreneurs who aspire to achieve great personal and professional success.

The author elaborates on his own journey of numerous failed business ventures which caused him to need to search for solutions to achieve his own entrepreneurial success.

If you are results focused and have big ambitions, but you are not reaching your potential, this book provides a proven five-step transformational process that the author has used as the basis to successfully coach over 1,000 of his paying clients.

The process has five steps:

Awaken awareness – becoming aware of the future you are currently headed for

Transformation – includes a detailed seven-step exercise for mindset transformation

Dream the dream – to clearly vision your ultimate desired future

Choose the dream – using *the future focused plan* system

Live the dream – the practice of maintaining an empowered mindset

The effectiveness of the author's transformational process is illustrated with confidentiality-adjusted case studies.

For best results, rather than read the book first and then go back and complete the exercises, the author strongly recommends you read the book in sequence and do each activity, thoroughly, real time without skipping ahead.

Dan Warburton is an entrepreneur, published author, international speaker and coach who pioneers using mindset transformation to enable professionals and entrepreneurs to fulfil their greatest ambitions.

For more information go to: www.danwarburton.com

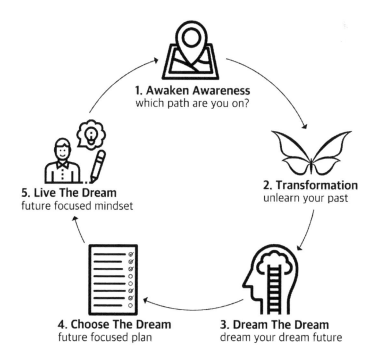

1. Awaken Awareness
which path are you on?

2. Transformation
unlearn your past

3. Dream The Dream
dream your dream future

4. Choose The Dream
future focused plan

5. Live The Dream
future focused mindset

Thank You
I Wouldn't Be Here Without You

"Success is only success when it can be shared."

~ Dan Warburton ~

Thank you Dad. You've always loved Mum so much and today you are a wonderful display of what it means to be faithful, loyal, understanding, compassionate and deeply loving. It's only because of all the amazing things you've done for me from taking care of me, guiding me and supporting me that I now get to live a lifestyle that I love so much.

I couldn't have wished for a better Dad.

Thank you Dad. I wouldn't be here without you.

Thank you Mum.

You've always been so extraordinarily loving. You are always the first to show kindness and a deep compassion towards others. No matter whether you address a beggar on the street or those to be seen as more privileged, you always speak from a place of being interested to know the person, to connect with them and see how you can serve them.

Your love and support has got me through the darkest of times and now I can thank you for the extraordinary life that I am now blessed to be able to live.

Thank you Mum. I wouldn't be here without you.

Thank you Chloe. As my sister it's wonderful to share this journey with you and I love seeing you also choosing a creative path.

I'm inspired to see how your new business venture works out.

You've always given me the opportunity to reflect and see how I can do more for you and in the process always refine my coaching and serving skills towards others.

Thank you Chloe. I wouldn't be here if it wasn't for you.

Thank you Damian. As my little brother you've shown me what true commitment and consistency looks like. You've become a solid pillar of strength for Laura and our beautiful little Ella. It's such an honour to be your brother and I can't wait to share more great times with you.

Thank you bro. I wouldn't be here without you.

Thank you Sofia, the divinely-hearted lady in my life. You virtually never complain, you are always serving me with amazing food, giving me healing treatments, kindness and so, so much love. You always make me feel so blessed to be alive. As I write this I am in tears, you really make my life so wonderful.

I love you with all my heart and I am loving sharing this journey so closely with you. Asking you to marry me – and marrying you – are the best choices I've ever made.

Thank you Lovely. I wouldn't be here if it wasn't for you.

Thank you Ben, my warm-hearted friend, for all the hours you have spent with me on the phone to exchange ideas and to guide me.

Thank you Ben. I wouldn't be here without you.

Thank you Keith, my wonderful friend, for all the profound coaching and healing you've given me. To this day, you are still the most intuitive coach and healer I know.

Your commitment to sharing your work is deeply inspirational. Taking on waking up the west to the powers of healing even in the face of so much resignation is extraordinary. You really do make the world a better place.

Thank you Keith. I wouldn't be here without you.

Thank you Sean Seah. As a mentor and guide to me, the knowledge you have given me has enabled me to succeed on a whole new level. Also, thank you so much for all the speaking opportunities you have created for me and for all the great connections you have introduced to me.

Thank you Sean. I wouldn't be here without you.

Thank you Elaine. As my PR agent and mentor who is guiding me through how to get my work to be enjoyed by many more, I cannot show my gratitude enough for your work and for what you've done for me. I am very inspired to be sharing this journey with you.

Thank you Elaine. I wouldn't be here without you.

Thank you Laura Rozenburga. There are many people in the world who are good at talking but can't prove their abilities. When it comes to social media marketing and strategies your skills stand out like a bright star.

I know no one else who is as skilled, knowledgeable and able to keep up with the evolutions of the internet like you. I am loving learning from you.

Thank you Laura. I wouldn't be here without you.

Thank you Skhu for showing me what it truly means to be grateful even amidst the most challenging of times. You've blessed me with great wisdom.

Thank you Skhu. I wouldn't be here without you.

Thank you Allar for being a great expression of what it means to be committed and open to growing and learning. I always love spending time with you and I look forward to more great times and collaborations ahead.

Thank you Allar. I wouldn't be here without you.

Thank you Harry for creating so many speaking opportunities for me, and for introducing me to so many wonderful people in your networks. It's because of you that I am now travelling all over the world as a successful speaker.

Thank you Harry. I wouldn't be here if it wasn't for you.

Thank you Hock Chong for all the speaking events we've partnered together to make happen and to make so successful. Because of our collaboration I've now created many new group coaching clients I've had the opportunity of serving and seeing rise to new heights as empowered human beings.

Thank you Hock Chong. I wouldn't be here if it wasn't for you.

Thank you to each and every one of you for giving me the gift of your attention, for attending my speaking events and listening. Thank you for buying this book, for registering into my programmes and for becoming my client. Thank you for sending me a smile and for everything you do, especially those little things that no one sees. You make the world a better place.

Thank you. I would not be here without you.

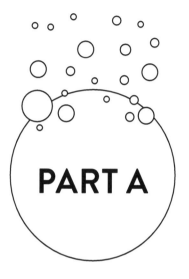

PART A

TRANSFORMATION FOR ENTREPRENEURS

Who Is Dan Warburton?

"To all of you who made fun of me, who bullied me, rejected me and laughed at me, I forgive you. You've made me unstoppable."

~ Dan Warburton ~

If you don't know much about me, you might be thinking who am I to be giving such bold information about transformation? Or how can I have the solution for you to break free of your unfulfilling situations and enable you to create your dream entrepreneur lifestyle?

These are all very reasonable questions.

I now have clients who through my coaching have become successful coaches, successful experts, A-list celebrity event organisers, high-level restaurant owners, high-performing sales experts, fashion label owners and many, many others now have businesses they love working in.

I am now regularly invited to speak on stages at events all over the world to share my knowledge of transformation and to speak about what transformation makes possible for professionals and entrepreneurs who are truly committed to living an extraordinary lifestyle.

My work particularly appeals to professionals, entrepreneurs, experts, business owners and coaches who want to make a great impact on the world, and in the process live a life of wealth and deep satisfaction in every area of their lives.

Over a 20-year period I've studied the art of self-transformation, mindset training and ontology (the study of being) as well as having read numerous books from many of the world's most influential people. I have also completed over 200 courses in self-development and spent the last ten years of my life consistently receiving coaching from at least one coach and sometimes from working with as many as five different coaches at once.

Through this commitment to developing myself I have transformed myself completely. As a result, I am now living my dream entrepreneur lifestyle.

I'm in great health. Every day I wake feeling inspiration and joy. I am extremely close to my family members.

I am also in a beautifully satisfying and loving relationship with the girl of my dreams whom I am soon to marry.

Virtually every day I get to wake up when I want and sleep when I want. I only need to work a few hours per week and these few hours feel like play.

I also have web spaces full of testimonials from professionals, likely just like you, stating that the quality of their lives has totally transformed through receiving my coaching, so I feel very much acknowledged and deeply rewarded for what I do for others.

I currently live in a luxury apartment with my fiancée in Malaysia. It has these amazing sea views from our balcony with the glittering lights of Singapore in the distance.

I also have plenty of money coming in to live a truly beautiful lifestyle, full of travel, adventure and a good balance of the finer things in life. In fact, we just got back from travelling to remote places in Indonesia where we walked along sandy white beaches, swam in crystal clear blue waters, went snorkelling over coral reefs and cruised by boat up rivers through rice fields and tropical forests.

The whole trip was absolutely breathtaking and unforgettable.

We have more trips booked to see other rural places across Asia. Later this year we are travelling across Europe where I plan to buy land and begin to work with architects to design and build our dream home with views over the Mediterranean Sea.

This is the idyllic lifestyle I live now, and my business is still effortlessly succeeding.

What made all this possible you might be wondering? All this was made possible by applying the secrets of transformation I'm going to reveal to you in this book.

If you want to experience living such a fulfilling lifestyle and entrepreneurial success, you need to understand what transformation is and how to apply it. I will guide you through the art of transformation and give you the opportunity of implementing the steps so you too can break free of your current circumstances and access a completely new and inspirational future.

This book is not based on fiction or theories I've heard from others but from my own hands-on experience applied both to my own life and from having observed many of my transformational coaching clients succeed in creating results they never imagined possible.

What I'm going to share with you in this book is real, proven and highly effective.

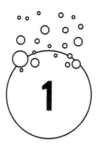

IS THIS BOOK FOR YOU?

"Only those who choose the dream can
live the dream."

~ Dan Warburton ~

Are you an entrepreneur... or do you want to be an entrepreneur?

Do you feel like you are not living your life to its full potential?

Are you bored or stuck at your current level?

Are you burned out?

Have you just broken up from a relationship or faced a business failure and are wondering what to do next?

Are you frustrated and just not producing the results you truly want?

Do you feel you have a major purpose but lack the courage to take action?

Are you currently in a dissatisfying employment position?

Do you feel alone and misunderstood because your ideas are too abstract for others to relate to?

Do you wish you could travel more?

Do you wish you were earning a lot more money?

Do you wish you could find a way of living your dream lifestyle by doing what you love?

Do you simply want to become super successful and impact the lives of many others in an inspirational way?

If *any* of these resonate with you, then yes, this is the perfect book for YOU.

A FINAL WARNING

"Seeing your fear and unlearning its cause is the secret to creating your dream lifestyle."

~ Dan Warburton ~

I have carefully crafted this book to guide you as a professional and entrepreneur to becoming honest with yourself and to discover ways of being that no longer serve you.

If you are truly serious about creating and living your dream lifestyle, I want you to realise that the only reason for reading this book is because you are not living the lifestyle you desire.

The truth is, the ways of being you have chosen to operate from until today have caused you to create everything you are currently experiencing, whether satisfying or not.

You might be experiencing earning less money than you are capable of. You might have unfulfilling business or personal relationships. Maybe you have a feeling of not impacting the world in any meaningful way. Maybe you are stuck in an employment job you don't enjoy. Whatever your circumstances, they are all an outcome of how you've been being in the past.

I understand this might be difficult to accept. You may feel you have all sorts of reasons outside yourself to explain your situation. Factors such as your upbringing, your environment, your government, a disability or some kind of a learning difficulty might seem like the cause of the life you live now. However harsh this may sound, this book will demonstrate that you are the cause of **everything** you are currently experiencing.

If you want a new, inspirational future you need to unlearn the causes of what has made you think, feel and behave in the ways you have in the past. If you don't take on new ways of being, you'll continue to operate in the same ways of being and keep producing the same results again and again.

Some people get this and are ready to go. For others, it will take a new level of open-mindedness to fully comprehend where I'm coming from. If you read this book and implement what you learn, I promise you will experience deeply rewarding change.

If you don't want to change, if you prefer to stay at the same level of mediocrity, then please close this book and give it to someone else, as this process is not for you.

However, if you are truly committed to creating and living your dream entrepreneur lifestyle, you will need to create new ways of being that will likely cause disruption to your routines. You will change as a person and re-evaluate your life. You will take new actions and design a future beyond your imagination.

This is my final warning.

Your future is now powerfully in your own hands.

WHY HAVE I WRITTEN THIS BOOK?

"Inspire the masses to live their dreams
by living yours."

~ Dan Warburton ~

I have written this book because it makes me sad to see you, the professional or entrepreneur, not succeeding at the high levels you are capable of, or even worse, struggling, failing and giving up.

I see all variations of underperforming, failure and defeat when coaching both professionals and entrepreneurs. You may be one of the few who is succeeding. However, I speak to countless ambitious individuals who are capable of achieving much greater things and impacting the world in a way that would reward them so much more.

I've coached lawyers, property investors, yoga teachers, therapists, coaches, mentors, speakers, healers, CEOs, artists, singers, authors, retreat organisers, business owners, traders, sales professionals, mediators, event organisers, elite beauticians and celebrities. All of them had one thing in common: their life was not what they wanted. The major frustration was an unsatisfactory level of business success and inability to impact the world in a profound way.

This book is the culmination of wisdom gained through putting myself through absolute hell in my quest to create and live an extraordinarily fulfilling, dream entrepreneur lifestyle. I've failed in making over 30 business ideas succeed. I've been bankrupt and lived in absolute poverty. At times I didn't even have any central heating in the bleak British winters. I was freezing cold and didn't know how I was going to buy food, let alone pay the rent for my tiny flat. I endured this hardship for years before succeeding in living the extraordinary lifestyle that I do now.

I am now committed to enabling professional individuals like you with big ambitions to not go through what I did and to enable you to succeed in a much shorter period of time than I did. With the right guidance you can create results far beyond what you imagine you are capable of.

Primarily I enable my entrepreneurial clients to create such extraordinary results through leading one-to-one transformational coaching conversations. However, I'm frustrated at not getting this incredibly powerful knowledge out there fast enough! There are still so many professionals and entrepreneurs out there, possibly you, who are not getting the level of satisfaction you deserve from all the hard effort you've put in, or you are simply struggling to get truly satisfying results.

The truth is, I'd absolutely love to see you, the committed professional or entrepreneur, succeed. I'd very much love to have the opportunity of sharing your success with you. Nothing fulfils me more than when my coaching clients share news of their extraordinary success with me. This makes me go to sleep every night with an amazing warmth in my heart and a sense that I'm living my greatest purpose while here on our planet Earth. It's a feeling I want you to feel every day too, because there is nothing more profoundly rewarding than this feeling.

If you read this book and you gain some insights and implement what you learn then please send me a message so I may enjoy hearing of your success. Your success as an entrepreneur means everything to me.

Why? Not only because I'd love to see you enjoying a highly successful lifestyle but also because I clearly see that it is entrepreneurs who hold the key to creating a better world. Entrepreneurs are the leaders of innovation and problem solving. It's us who have the courage to solve our world's most pressing problems – and in the process make a profit that we can enjoy and share to further help and empower others.

If I empower you, the entrepreneur who genuinely wants to impact the world in a great way, I'll also be empowering the people you are connected to, many of whom could go on to create an even better world for us all. A commitment to such a mission causes an inspirational ripple effect.

I want to enable as many entrepreneurs, business owners and committed professionals as possible to live their dream lifestyle. Not to just think about it or only daydream about it but to actually live those dreams for real and along the way to also live a life full of joy, happiness, purpose, satisfaction and wealth on every level and area of their lives.

I've written this book to give professionals and entrepreneurs all the greatest insights I've gained from numerous years as a transformational coach specialising in empowering entrepreneurs to create and live their dream lifestyle.

If anything I say resonates with you, if you find yourself inspired or challenged, then read on, as these are signs you are growing. This book is for you, the committed professional or entrepreneur.

THE DREAM ENTREPRENEUR LIFESTYLE

"To continually light a path ahead even when amidst darkness and inspire others to do the same for themselves is the key to your greatest success."

~ Dan Warburton ~

What exactly do I mean by *The Dream Entrepreneur Lifestyle?* You need to clarify your reason for reading this book so you will take in this information effectively. So let's begin by ensuring we are clear on what I mean by the dream entrepreneur lifestyle.

In my favourite Robin Sharma book *The Monk Who Sold His Ferrari* is a paragraph that defines what I see as the dream entrepreneur lifestyle. He calls it happiness.

"The secret of happiness is simple: find out what you truly love to do and then direct all of your energy towards doing it. If you study the happiest, healthiest, most satisfied people of our world, you will see that each and every one of them has found their passion in life, and then spent their days pursuing it. This calling is almost always one that, in some way, serves others. Once you are concentrating your mind, power and energy on a pursuit that you love, abundance flows into your life, and all your desires are fulfilled with ease and grace."

The dream entrepreneur lifestyle is a lifestyle that can only be achieved through a sustained level of effort and consistent action. This way of being is only implemented by a very small percentage of professionals and entrepreneurs. This is because most ambitious individuals subconsciously battle disempowering views of themselves and the world. They live in a constant state of survival. Not only is this totally subconscious but most assume the way the world occurs to them is real and they ask themselves: "How on earth can I find the time to do what I enjoy if I can't even get out of the situation I'm in?"

So most settle for second best. They procrastinate. They stay in work roles they don't enjoy. They underprice themselves and they take on work they don't want to do. And they don't dream about the kind of lifestyle they'd love to create.

Consequently, they never take the required and consistent actions required to succeed. The outcome is that most endure an unsatisfactory lifestyle because they are lost in a mindset of automatically surviving their fears rather than simply creating their dream lifestyle.

Sad but true. The Oxford English Dictionary defines an entrepreneur as *'A person who sets up a business or businesses, taking on financial risks in the hope of profit.'*

I personally choose not to live a life of hope but rather to live a life of choosing and to consciously choose my destiny, then simply take consistent actions to create and tangibly live it. This aside, I am not only referring to the financial side of being an entrepreneur but also to the quality of life that being a business owner makes possible for you and others in the world.

Though it may not seem obvious, your focus is never the money, it is always about the lifestyle made possible through the money earned and the freedom made possible by being a business owner and entrepreneur. Our focus must be the end result otherwise we are as a ship lost out at sea without a destination to move towards and so we'll just drift until the day we die.

By the dream entrepreneur lifestyle I mean a life of wealth on every level including financial wealth, health wealth, relationship wealth and most of all living a lifestyle that leaves us feeling deeply satisfied on a daily basis.

Such a satisfying lifestyle can only be experienced if we feel we are elevating not only our own life but also the lives of others effectively. As Robin Sharma states: "This calling is almost always one that, in some way, serves others." Sadly, most are not awakened enough to realise that there is nothing more unfulfilling than becoming financially wealthy and then not enjoying sharing the wealth with others, being free but not having anyone to share that freedom with, or being healthy while witnessing so many others in the world suffer from diseases.

Equally it's clear from my coaching of professionals and from observing myself that the minute we sense that what we're doing is making someone else's life better, we feel a deep sense of satisfaction, and when my clients start the transformational coaching process most of them soon realise that their highest aspiration is to master wealth in every area of their life. Then they quickly realise that they want that overall wealth to also elevate the lives of others around them.

If you master this, you will be living a lifestyle that is both full of wealth and deeply satisfying.

You'll awaken every day feeling truly inspired. This is what I call *The Dream Entrepreneur Lifestyle.*

MY PROFOUND TRANSFORMATIONAL AWAKENING

"Mastery is not being who you think you are, it's being who you need to be to create the future you choose."

~ Dan Warburton ~

Though I'm now living an extraordinary lifestyle, it's taken me years to find the secret to breaking through the self-imposed limitations that were previously causing me to struggle in every area of my life including health, relationships and finances.

All my life I've been very ambitious. My parents would often tell me I was being overly ambitious. "Be realistic!" my mum would often sternly say to me while I was growing up as a teenager. Even so I couldn't help myself from telling everyone about the dreams

I so deeply yearned to realise. Deep down I also wanted to make my father proud, but no matter what I tried I could never seem to achieve this.

In my teenage years I found that being in a full-time employment position caused me to feel like I was a slave. Being employed felt like I had to live my life based on someone else's terms and not on those of my own. You name a job and I tried it from being a paper delivery boy, flipping buns in McDonald's, cutting grass for the council, packing CDs in a CD factory, sweeping away tons of shot-blast sand from car parks ready for renovation, moving building materials by hand in freezing cold winters, and even night shifts washing dishes in restaurants at Gatwick Airport. You name it, I tried it and I hated it.

Later into my 20s I began to dream of being able to become financially successful by only doing work that I truly enjoyed. I began trying to build up my name as a high-level DJ and was also offering my interior design skills, that I'd gained while at university, to clothing shop owners. Neither of these things earned any decent amount of money for me and so I had to continue working on building sites.

By the age of 30, every area of my life was extremely unsatisfactory. As time went on, I clearly saw how all the areas of our lives are closely interlinked. If one area is out of balance, the rest soon also become unbalanced and unsatisfactory.

By this age I was fearing having to face a life of dealing with Britain's employment and financial systems which left me feeling very depressed. I could see that it was likely that I was facing a mediocre existence, one of full-time employment, paying taxes, no freedom and one day death. This deeply angered me yet it also made me dream bigger than ever. I was determined to not end up living a mediocre existence as most around me were.

I dreamed of buying land in southern Europe, designing and building my dream home with sea views, owning a supercar, travelling, speaking on stages all over the world, inspiring millions of other people to also do whatever it takes to live a fulfilling lifestyle and all the while generating great financial wealth.

As I got older I became aware that what I also really wanted was to make my father feel proud of me. He'd always been so loving, so caring and in truth he was my idol. He's an outstanding man who is the leader of a highly successful business specialising in transport providers and resellers' ticketing solutions. He's always earned enough to provide for all our family and grown in financial success. He also bought and renovated a beautiful Victorian house in the affluent countryside of Sussex in England.

Dad has always been faithful to my mum and a devoted father. He's incredibly reliable, impeccably organised and even in his late 70s goes to the gym at 6am three times a week.

Yet no matter what I did or how hard I tried, I kept producing the same failing results and could never impress him, or so it seemed make him proud of me.

By my early 30s I'd managed to become self-employed and I was my own boss. I called myself *Super Dan the Handy Man!* I offered all sorts of handy jobs and repairs that I carried out for people on their homes and did them all off the back of a retro, 1987 Honda CBX750F motorcycle. They were somewhat fun days as I'd manage to consistently earn enough to at least pay my own way but I still couldn't earn anywhere near enough to buy my own home or land, so I felt the only solution was to offer more services and start employing people.

Five years ago I thought I'd gone up in the world when I moved into a slightly larger flat. It was in an old Victorian hotel in the fun city of Brighton called The Abbey Hotel. My front-facing suite had one tiny bathroom with no daylight, one tiny kitchen and one room for everything else (a table, a sofa and my bed). It was a very quirky place. I felt like I was staying in a bed and breakfast on permanent holiday in a seaside town.

My main room had amazing high ceilings and huge windows that allowed the light to flood in. But these original 100-year-old windows had big gaps around them that let in freezing cold air. And there was no central heating.

English winters consist of grey, rainy, damp and very, very cold days that often felt as if they'd go on endlessly. I often felt so cold that I couldn't focus on solving the most simple task. No matter how empowered I thought I was in withstanding such cold, I could never fully relax.

While living in this place I was trying to make one of my many business ideas succeed. On this occasion it was a property renovations business. I had grown my business from being just me as Super Dan to the leader of Team Super. I had a team of eight people working full-time and though from the outside it looked like I was succeeding, I couldn't afford to pay my rent and was too embarrassed to ask my dad to borrow more money again.

I remember one freezing cold Sunday in February 2015. It was so cold in my flat that I could see the steam of my breath. It was lunchtime and I was kneeling on the kitchen floor as I looked in my fridge to see what I had to eat. All I had was some broccoli and half an onion.

The onion had turned mouldy but the broccoli was fine. While wearing my three thick, torn jumpers I put the broccoli in a pan with some water then placed it on the electric hob to boil. As it boiled, I warmed my fingers in the steam that rose from the water.

I felt lost. I'd tried it all and had failed at it all. Most of over 30 business ideas I'd worked on I'd never managed to get off the ground, or those that did failed within a year. I'd tried becoming an interior designer for shop owners, offering personal stylist services to wealthy people and massage therapy to people who were stressed. I'd tried making it as a DJ for years, which was great fun but this never earned any kind of decent money. I bought and sold silver bullion and at one point I even sold second-hand vacuum cleaners! These were just a handful of the business ideas I tried. None of them ever became truly financially successful.

I was worrying about being late in paying my rent for over three weeks. I didn't know what I was going to tell my landlord. I was terrified. I just didn't know what to try next. The property maintenance business I'd built up over two years was clearly on track to fail, as all my other business ideas.

Truth is I'd rather have been homeless than move back into my parents' house. I couldn't face the shame of having to do that as a failed entrepreneur. I was also never going to work for an employer again as I'd had enough of being exploited, underpaid and told what to do or when I could or couldn't go on holiday.

This time I was in a particularly confronting situation because I had weekly wages to pay to eight staff members and clients with outstanding building works. My clients kept calling me to complain about the mistakes my workmen made. To keep my clients happy I used credit cards to pay other building repair companies to fix the jobs my workmen messed up. I knew it was entirely my fault as I was accepting projects for my team far beyond their skills.

This left me hitting an overdraft limit on six credit cards as well as on two personal accounts and my business bank account. I could feel fear build up inside me, heat in my stomach and anger over my situation.

I gritted my teeth hard as I gazed into the water boiling in the pan on my stove. A deep determination rose through me. I must find a way out of my situation and succeed, I thought.

At this time I was also participating in a two-year-long self-development programme that focused on transformational-based team management and leadership skills.

The next day I used my last bit of cash to buy a train ticket to London for my weekly leadership training session. I was then sat in the training centre before my class was to start and I asked my coach why I was constantly struggling financially and failing in business.

My coach began to ask me some powerful questions such as what was I secretly frightened of happening? As we got deeper into the coaching conversation I began to remember something that happened to me when I was very young. What I discovered was the greatest realisation of my life.

I remembered being sat on the left-hand side of a double pushchair with my brother sat in the right-hand seat. He was one year old and I was three. It was a bright sunny day and my mum had walked into a shop to buy something. When she came out I raised my arms up towards her so she could give me what she'd bought but she seemed to ignore me and gave it to my brother. I couldn't believe what was happening. This thing called my brother had taken all the love and attention away from me and had ruined my life. This made me extremely angry, so to get my revenge I bit his ear. He screamed and screamed and cried and cried as he flung his arms and legs around.

My father saw what happened and ran over to me and, pointing his finger at me, in a stern voice said, "You don't do that to your brother. He's your brother! You should love your brother." While this was happening my brother was getting even more attention from my mum as she was now cuddling him to make him feel better from me biting his ear.

Re-living this moment in my mind, I remembered feeling my brother had taken everything away from me, that my mum loved my brother and not me. Also while my mum was comforting my brother, my father was shouting at me. Then people passing by began to stare at me being sternly disciplined by my father, which left me feeling very embarrassed.

I suddenly became aware of what I was thinking in that moment and that was, I'm not good enough, nobody wants me.

With more skilled questioning from my coach and further reflection on this pivotal event, I realised that in this moment in that pushchair at the age of three I thought I'd discovered that the world was *I'm just not good enough, nobody wants me.*

Becoming aware of this invented view or belief I formed during this emotional moment was the catalyst for transformation so profound that even today, eight years later, I'm still enjoying the extraordinary benefits. I am only able to live my current lifestyle because of this key realisation.

I realised that ever since this event at the age of three I had spent virtually my whole life operating and reacting because of this subconscious way of viewing myself. I finally became aware that not only did I have this fundamental way of thinking behind everything I did but that *I'm just not good enough, nobody wants me* was a totally subconscious interpretation (or view) I'd invented about myself and the world.

Everything I'd done since this event at the age of three was motivated by making sure I was never seen as *not good enough* and *unwanted*. At all cost, I was driven to make sure I was always seen as *good enough* and *wanted* by everyone at all times.

Within minutes of having this insight I felt exposed, like I could no longer hide behind my act and use manipulative ploys to be seen as good enough and wanted by others. I was shocked to my absolute core and was left speechless as the realisation deepened and resonated in every fibre of my body.

I could see why at school I was so obsessed with looking good and gaining everyone's approval. I also realised why I'd tried to become a superstar DJ and why I was more concerned that my team were wearing matching uniforms to mine than the financial stability of the business.

I also saw why I'd get so nervous in interviews and why I'd find it so difficult to ask a girl out on a date. I saw why I worked so hard and for such long hours which often caused me to burn myself out. And why I procrastinated about trying new solutions when things were failing.

It was all because I was on a deeply reactive mission to ensure that no one would ever discover that *I am not good enough* and that *nobody wants me.*

Realising what my future was going to be like if I carried on being *I am not good enough, nobody wants me* shocked me. This shock caused me to awaken out of this self-destructive view of myself and the world.

I saw that if I carried on procrastinating, avoiding, playing small, always saying things just to look good rather than being honest, while constantly putting on a false demonstration of being the big businessman without having true structures in place, I was headed for more failure and much worse. I was headed for a life of deep regret and despair. Yet until this moment I was totally oblivious to this.

The fundamental freedom I gained from becoming aware of this previously subconscious way of thinking was understanding that this once destructive mantra of *I am not good enough, nobody wants me* was simply something that I invented, and nothing more. I instantly saw that ever since this event as a toddler I'd been assuming that my invention of *I am not good enough, nobody wants me* was a reality.

Finally, I awakened out of this false view of the world that from the age of three and up until that moment I thought I had to cope with and survive. The weight just lifted off my shoulders, I felt my back relax upright as a sensation of lightness and freedom arose through me.

My disempowering, fundamental yet subconscious view of myself which was *I am not good enough, nobody wants me* explained why during my 20s and early 30s I struggled to get even one business up and running successfully.

Previously, I was also so paralysed with fear about what people thought of me, I was afraid of being honest and just saying I don't know when I didn't have an answer. I hoped that every action I took would get me noticed and gain the recognition I yearned for. I was so terrified of being disliked by others that I'd say whatever I imagined they wanted to hear to win approval. This people-pleasing made me come across as needy especially when trying to close a sale.

I realised that before I was more preoccupied by what others thought of me rather than being focused on taking the actions that really mattered. Ever since this breakthrough realisation my life began to change in an extraordinary and wonderful way.

I gave up my DJ-ing career, which truthfully was draining me, and instead began to take actions that were actually responsible, calculated, consistent and best of all, effective at bringing me closer to living my dream entrepreneur lifestyle.

While closing down my property maintenance business, a very demanding time, I successfully launched a new business in partnership with a businessman who had a team of skilled building repair specialists and plumbers. We created a new business offering a range of services from building repairs, plastering and decorating as well as emergency plumbing and drainage services.

I never had to pick up any tools or manage anyone else ever again. Instead of having to manage a big team of workmen, I simply closed the sales. I did this by walking into the local letting agencies in Brighton, introducing myself and informing them about our services. Before long my phone began to ring constantly with enquiries. I'd answer the calls, close the sales, then texted the details to my business partner who managed everything involved with the delivery of the work. He'd then simply let me know each month how much to invoice him for and *voilà!* The money was in my bank account.

It was virtually effortless as I simply needed to place a few advertisements in local magazines, go out networking every so often, and the rest of the time I could focus on my self-development training and go out and party. That year I went to more music festivals and travelled more than I'd ever travelled in one year. I stayed in luxury resorts and went snowboarding in the Alps. I attended seven long weekend music festivals and went on beach holidays in southern Europe.

At last, the good times had arrived and I was having so much fun! It was amazing and things quickly got even better as reputation of our service grew.

Later, when I was 38, I was at my parents' home in their beautiful little village in Sussex where I'd grown up throughout my teenage years and my father had noticed that not only was I centred and calm, I was also properly succeeding in business. He knew this because I hadn't asked him to lend me any money for over a year and I'd paid him back most of what I owed.

While we stood side by side in the kitchen as my father enjoyed his Italian espresso coffee, we both looked out of the window across the beautiful green countryside on a warm day in summer. For the first time, there was a beautiful peacefulness between us. Before this I'd always argue and need to be right. Or I'd need to have the last word, or be seen by him to be good enough and wanted. However, because of my transformational awakening, I no longer needed these illusive cravings to be fulfilled by him to make me feel like I'd made him proud of me, because for the first time in my life I was free of seeing myself as *not good enough or not wanted.*

Because of this new calmness in me, he broke the silence and asked, after about seven years of me telling him about my transformational based studies, "So, what is this transformational thing you do?"

"Why don't we sit down and I can tell you about it?" I replied. He agreed and within an hour we were both sitting at the corner of his desk in his office.

My father carefully took a sip of his hot cup of tea, then sat back and became totally still as he made eye contact with me. I could tell that he was very interested as to what I was going to say next. I'd never seen him being like this towards me before.

By this time I'd acquired years of practice in coaching other attendees of the self-development courses I was participating in. I had developed a real skill in guiding others to have breakthrough insights (like I'd had) by enabling them to also become aware of how they subconsciously viewed themselves and the world.

I explained to my father about transformation and how it worked. I could see my father was becoming fascinated about what self-transformation could make possible because he kept asking me more questions.

Soon I led the conversation for my dad to look at his own lifestyle and bit by bit the conversation became heated. Dad sat back on his chair with his arms folded telling me how he had everything he wanted in his life and wished for nothing more. He was certain that he was happy and didn't need anything else.

As we both faced each other I said, "Dad, I get that you feel happy and I get that you've reached a point where you own this beautiful house, you have a wonderful family and you feel you need nothing more. However, you don't know why you wake up every day."

I went on to tell him how he's on autopilot and just wakes up every day to do what he needs to do because his business relies on him. He believes he has no choice but to do the daily grind and feels enslaved by his business.

"Dad, you spend your life surviving and not creating because you don't know why you wake up each day," I said to him in a direct manner.

At this point he sat upright. "You are a youngster, you have no idea, you can't tell me that!" he replied in a stern voice.

Because of the transformational awakening I'd gone through I no longer felt the need to be reactive towards him as I used to. I no longer felt compelled to have my father be in a certain way to counteract my old story of *I'm just not good enough, nobody wants me* because I was no longer dominated by that old way of viewing myself.

Instead, I was able to be still and fully listen to him, to fully hear my father without the need to defend myself or even reply. Instead, for the first time in my life, as my father got angry towards me I was able to hold the silence. Because of this and how I gave him the space to be outspoken, he then also became silent.

He held a quiet pause while gazing at me then said, "Crikey! You are right, I have spent my life surviving. Bloody hell, sunshine! You're very good at this!"

In that moment the way we identified to each other, me seeing him as my father and him seeing me as his son, vanished. In that moment we were nothing more than human-to-human, best friends and soul mates. I could see the deep layers of illusionary definition my father had about me lift from his mind. My father awoke to see me for the man I'd become as a result of 15 years in intense self-development. For the first time, because I didn't defend myself and instead was able to give my father space to think and reflect, he understood me and saw that I was not the desperate little boy I used to be.

It was as if I had a contract sent down from the universe that read: Now that you can coach your father, you can coach anyone. Signed, God!

It was another profound and life-transforming moment for me because I then no longer feared my father. This absence of fear towards the man I looked up to more than anyone had an amazing ripple effect where from then on I was able to powerfully hold myself still, calm and poised in any conversation with any other person in any time, in any place.

This level of skill in communication is vital for a coach to be able to coach another effectively. Yet most coaches I meet have not done the deep inner work on themselves to enable such a skilled level of communication in their coaching. This then causes them to lose their train of thought, to not listen or get defensive during a coaching conversation. When this happens, the coach becomes highly ineffective and the client doesn't gain any new insights.

Sadly, the world is full of people claiming to be a coach. Many have expensive qualifications to prove they are skilled at coaching. Yet they haven't even healed their relationship to those they love such as their parents, brothers, sisters, friends, colleagues and neighbours. So it baffles me as to how they think they can effectively coach anyone else to overcome their relationship or business challenges.

My father went on to ask me, "Have you ever thought about doing this professionally?"

"Well actually Dad," I replied, "I've had two other people this month tell me that I should become a professional coach so you know what, I'm going to go for it."

And so, in January 2016, that's what I did. Though I had years of experience in coaching others participating in self-development courses led by other organisations, I launched myself as a professional coach and began winding down all my other businesses. Within three months I grew a successful coaching practice and have been in demand ever since.

As a result of this conversation with my father, I gained his respect and I was shocked when he requested that I give him regular coaching sessions! I couldn't believe it, my father was asking me for advice! He soon became one of my first coaching clients and as a result of my coaching he has now managed to grow his ferry boat ticket reservation business to a whole new level of success.

I ended up guiding my father through a challenging business restructuring period and now his business is in the best shape ever. Not only this, my father now has the business he's always wanted where he can work as much or as little as he likes with plenty of time to relax and enjoy life. Having put my father through hell as an impossible teenager, it was deeply satisfying to heal our relationship and give back to him something that's made a real and lasting difference to the quality of his life. Even today I still can't believe that my own father, my dad, still approaches me for business advice and coaching!

All this only became possible because of the transformation I'd gone through. I no longer needed to survive such disempowering ways of thinking because I'd unlearned the thought patterns that put me in survival mode. Instead I could confidently introduce myself, set up appointments, make effective business proposals and close sales.

Now, nearly three years later, between one-to-one and small group coaching sessions I've coached over 1,000 individuals made up of committed professionals and entrepreneurs. My website is also now full of testimonials from both professionals and entrepreneurs stating that they have achieved results that they never imagined possible.

What many of my clients say in their testimonials is so extraordinary that I've had to feature a link to their web page so anyone can write and confirm if what they say about me and my coaching is really true.

Word is now out about the results my clients achieve so I'm often invited to speak on stage at events with sizeable audiences around the world about what transformation makes possible for entrepreneurs who truly want to create and live their dream lifestyle.

I've recently moved to Singapore to fulfil regular speaking slots across Asia. I'm having so much fun it's crazy. As I write this I'm actually on a plane back to England to see my family for Christmas then I'm going snowboarding in the Alps again with my friend Keith. In the next few months I'm speaking at events across Asia, then Dubai then flying back to the UK to speak at other events there.

While managing the logistics around my speaking career I have a manageable number of one-to-one coaching clients and my group coaching courses are sold out. Just two years ago, I never imagined I'd be living this high-level and adventurous lifestyle.

I can't even begin to describe how fulfilling my life is now. I don't need to worry about money or not having enough time. I also have the freedom and resources to travel, to do all the things I've always dreamed of doing and to share all this with the people I love. Best of all, the work I do truly impacts the lives of professionals and entrepreneurs in a wonderful way and I'm regularly thanked and acknowledged for the difference my coaching makes. I feel so blessed and deeply grateful.

I owe a heartfelt thank you to everyone who has made this lifestyle possible. Also you reading this book is a great honour and a gift from you to me. I can't thank you enough.

Because of the profound transformational insights I've gained through skilled coaching, I'm now living this extraordinarily fulfilling lifestyle, but to get here took me years of struggling.

Now I want to empower every professional and entrepreneur I can, including you, to awaken from any subconscious and disempowering views that may be holding you back from creating and living your dream entrepreneur lifestyle. This book is aimed at enabling you, the entrepreneur (or aspiring entrepreneur), to free yourself of your past, to take new and powerful actions, and access a completely new and inspirational future.

Because of how I struggled for years, I now want to guide as many other ambitious individuals as possible who are truly committed to succeed to also achieve this for real. Nothing fulfils me more than seeing ambitious entrepreneurs succeed and being able to celebrate their success with them.

This is why I've written this book.

In this book I am going to reveal to you my life's greatest insights and key observations that I've gained from having enabled numerous professionals and entrepreneurs to create extraordinary results. I am going to break down what reflection transformation is and why it really is the secret to creating the dream entrepreneur lifestyle.

Once you understand this you'll be left with a clear understanding of surviving versus creating and of how the survival parts of your brain work. You'll get to unlearn the subconscious ways of thinking that likely cause you to procrastinate and play small, you'll become clear in how to move forward and you'll find the courage to take powerful and bold new actions.

You will be empowered and guided in how to create and live your dream entrepreneur lifestyle, for real.

THE SUBCONSCIOUS REFLECTION CREATION TRAP

"We all end up creating a reflection of what we think we are. Transform this thought-based invention and you'll be able to create a completely new future."

~ Dan Warburton ~

My whole life's research and development based on nearly 15 years in coaching has led me to this one central universal rule that applies to us humans and it is this:

We all create a reflection of what we think we are and are not.

Let me explain what I mean.

As an entrepreneur, it is your subconscious views (interpretations) that you have of yourself and the world around you that determine the results (or lack of them) that you create because they dominate your every action and non-action.

As the famous quote by Henry Ford states: *"Whether you think you can, or you think you can't – you're right."*

So, what does Ford mean by this?

This means that if you don't think you can succeed at something you won't even try. And in not trying no results will be created so you will prove to yourself that you cannot succeed. While the opposite is also true: if you think you can succeed at something then it's likely you'll get into action. You'll then see some rewarding results appear and will be much more likely to succeed. You'll create a reflection of *I can*.

This is what I mean by *we all create a reflection of what we think we are and are not.*

Apart from the circumstances you're born into, fundamentally all the results you have in your life right now are a result of how you've been being in the past.

Being meaning: saying, communicating and all actions and non-actions you've taken up to today. This applies to your finances, the house you live in, your health, your relationships and of course to the level of success or lack of success you are currently experiencing in one or more areas of your life.

To quote Book 3 of the trilogy series *Conversations With God* by Neale Donald Walsh:

"We talked about the Be-Do-Have paradigm, and how most people have it reversed. Most people believe if they have a thing (more time, money, love, whatever), then they can finally do a thing (write a book, take up a hobby, go on vacation, buy a home, undertake a relationship), which will allow them to be a thing (happy, peaceful, content or in love).

"In actuality, they are reversing the Be-Do-Have paradigm. In the universe as it really is (as opposed to how you likely think it is) *havingness* does not produce *beingness*, but the other way round.

"First you be the thing called *happy* (or knowing or wise or compassionate, or whatever); then you start *doing* things from this place of being-ness and soon you discover that what you are doing winds up bringing you the things you've always wanted."

I totally agree with these concepts and I find that most entrepreneurs are being in ways that are simply not effective for creating the truly satisfying results they want in life. Most entrepreneurs are being chasing, wanting, needy, yearning, avoiding or unappreciative and the kind of results that such ways of being are likely to create are never fulfilling.

So, it makes absolute sense that to truly succeed we must primarily focus on how we are *being*. We must transform an ineffective way of being into an effective way of being especially in regard to creating your ultimate entrepreneur lifestyle.

The cause of how you are being is dominated by what you think you are and are not. So, we must firstly transform such thinking to enable you to then access and be in a new and effective way.

Nearly every single entrepreneur and professional I've coached through my *7 Point Transformational Mandala System* awakened to becoming aware of a disempowering interpretation of themselves and the world around them. This was previously subconsciously holding them back when it came to successfully creating fulfilling results.

If you find yourself procrastinating, avoiding, playing small, settling for second best, feeling burned out, overworking, feeling bored or uninspired then the cause of these states of being are disempowering views that you are subconsciously carrying about yourself and the world around you. These views are dominating you and causing you to be in such ineffective ways.

I boldly state this based on my clear observation from having coached over 1,000 entrepreneurs, many of whom were previously suffering from such limiting *states of being.*

Those who have attended a deep transformational session with me but didn't become aware of such an interpretation were so clouded by disempowering views of themselves they couldn't become clear enough to actually awaken from the trance. This was like me trying to convince a fish that it's been in water all its life. Some just don't have the courage to admit what they have been swimming in all their lives.

Sometimes entrepreneurs are just not willing to open their minds enough to see how they are getting in the way of themselves. It's impossible to see a blind spot while in it. Insight comes when you awaken and look at yourself from the outside. Some clients were simply not ready to admit that the creator of all their unsatisfactory circumstances was *themselves.* Instead they tried to antagonise me to become reactionary so they could argue they were right and prove me wrong. I've had to walk away from such conversations.

At times even my most skilled coaching couldn't help them and sadly there was nothing I could do other than let them carry on down a path of mere survival and dissatisfaction. Fortunately, this has only happened on a very few occasions.

Through my coaching, the subconscious, self-inflicted disempowering views that most entrepreneurs became aware of were:

- I'm not good enough

- I don't fit in

- I'm weak

- I'm alone

- I'm invisible

- I don't belong here

- I'm second best

- I'm different

- I'm not wanted

- I'm not loved

- I'm abandoned

- I'll never succeed

- I can't do it

The commonality between all these views is that they all start with I as in their self-concept and identity. In the majority of cases when entrepreneurs become aware of such subconscious, disempowering interpretations of themselves, they also become aware of the origins. These beliefs usually begin in childhood from an experience of being scared, embarrassed, abused, violated or particularly challenged in some way.

These shaping events are not necessarily extremely traumatic but unavoidable life experiences such as being shouted at by parents, moving home as a child, starting a new school, seeing parents divorce or being laughed at and teased at school. These are the kind of events you might also have experienced where the survival part of your brain interpreted how you perceived the world in that pivotal moment.

What happens is the reptilian part of our brain, the part that handles survival, simply does its thing. It gets heavily involved when we experience a particularly deep emotional challenge then attempts to save us by interpreting the incident with seemingly accurate information on what to think and do to survive.

Below you can see a diagram where you, the entrepreneur, are standing on the left and your world is on the right. The top arrow (numbered 1) stands for the views you have of yourself and how you act out or be in the face of your world.

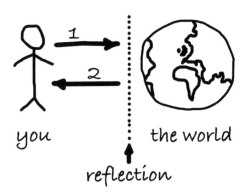

Whether these views be empowering or disempowering they subconsciously give expectations of what you think you'll receive back from the world in the form of results from the actions you take.

In other words, if you think I can, I'm unstoppable or I'll find a way then you'll take action and the world will likely reflect back rewarding results. On the other hand, if you think I'm not good enough, I'll fail or I'll never succeed then you'll likely not take any sort of big or bold action and thus these views will then be reflected back at you in a lack of rewarding results.

The second arrow (numbered 2) stands for the feedback or the reflection of the kind of views you originally have about yourself that you experience in your world.

The impacts of any subconscious disempowering interpretation that you may have about yourself is absolutely disastrous on the quality of your lifestyle especially as an entrepreneur.

At the end of this chapter is a table that demonstrates the effects of this.

In the left-hand column are the disempowering interpretations that you may subconsciously have of yourself. The second column shows the kind of actions or non-actions you might be taking because of such views. The third column shows the results you are likely to get from these actions/non-actions and finally the fourth column shows the disempowering view of yourself and the world that is 'proved' to be true.

As you will see from the table below this overview of the general ways we human beings survive such interpretations is fairly straightforward.

The table gives you a sense of the kind of actions and non-actions such interpretations may be causing you to take (or not take), then as a consequence the results or lack of results that you would tend to experience. Finally, those kinds of results or a lack of them only ever prove to ourselves that what we think we are and are not really is true.

My conclusion stands: *we all create a reflection of what we think we are and are not.*

This is a vicious trap that has a profoundly damaging impact on the quality of your entrepreneurial lifestyle where no matter how much harder you work or how many times you try starting something new or how many new employment positions you try, you are only left creating and experiencing the same unfulfilling experiences again and again.

The impact of this is that one day you will wake up with deep sadness and regret that you haven't lived your life to its greatest potential. The solution to freeing yourself from this trap is to become aware of these subconscious and disempowering interpretations then to transform them.

It's the process of transforming such disempowering ways of thinking that I'll be covering in this book which has now enabled so many of my clients to become highly empowered and as a result of this succeed in creating results they never imagined possible.

You can practise the process for yourself later in this book.

1. The Disempowering Interpretation (How you are being the face of your world)	I'm not good enough.
2. The Action / Non-Action	To avoid others finding out that you might just be not good enough you avoid taking action in case you fail. Or you keep yourself busy to show others you are trying very hard but ensure the actions you take keep you busy in safe roles and nothing more. Or you take big actions, get some good results, maybe burn yourself out, then change your mind saying I don't feel like it anymore and start something new. Or you get bored easily and continuously start something new.
3. The Results or Lack of Results	No results. Nothing happens. You feel unhappy and regretful that time is passing you by and you don't accomplish everything. You stay in an unfulfilling work position, you play small and stay safe in a repetitive routine. You go through highs of celebration and then lows of disappointment because the results are only temporarily fulfilling. A feeling of lasting success never seems to be possible. You end up feeling disappointed, burned out or both.
4. The Disempowering Interpretation that gets proved as true (The reflection we experience back from the world)	I'm not good enough.

1. The Disempowering Interpretation (How you are being the face of your world)	I'm abandoned.
2. The Action / Non-Action	In case you fail and thus be abandoned again you simply avoid this possibly happening again by not taking any actions. Or you keep yourself busy doing things to please others to ensure you are not abandoned and end up neglecting your own wishes. Or you take big actions to win the approval of others to ensure not being abandoned. You get some results but then in fearing failing and being abandoned you don't commit fully, you don't operate at your full potential to avoid the chance of experiencing failing and avoid possibly being abandoned again.
3. The Results or Lack of Results	No results. Nothing happens. You feel unhappy and regretful that time is passing you by and you don't accomplish anything particularly satisfying. You stay in an unfulfilling work position, you play small and stay safe in a repetitive routine while feeling angry at others for why you can never seem to succeed. You go through highs of celebration and then lows of disappointment because the results are only temporarily fulfilling if ever at all. A feeling of lasting success doesn't seem possible. You end up feeling exhausted.
4. The Disempowering Interpretation that gets proved as true (The reflection we experience back from the world)	I'm abandoned.

1. The Disempowering Interpretation (How you are being the face of your world)	I'm not loved.
2. The Action / Non-Action	In case you fail and thus find out that you really are not loved you just avoid the possibility of experiencing this by not taking any kind of focused action. Or you keep yourself busy doing things for others to gain love. You don't care for your own needs so well and burn yourself out while doing things you don't want to do just to try and gain love or approval from others. Or you take big actions to get love from others, you get some good results then in fearing failing and losing peoples love you change your mind saying I have a better way to become successful and continuously start something new before truly succeeding.
3. The Results or Lack of Results	No results. Nothing happens. You feel unhappy and regretful that time is passing you by and you feel sad because of not accomplishing anything satisfying. You stay in an unfulfilling work position, you play small and stay safe in a repetitive routine. You end up frustrated that you can never seem to succeed in your own commitments. You go through highs of celebration and then lows of disappointment because the results are only temporarily fulfilling. A feeling of being recognised for your abilities and creating lasting success doesn't seem possible. You are left feeling resigned and like nothing will ever change.
4. The Disempowering Interpretation that gets proved as true (The reflection we experience back from the world)	I'm not loved.

WILL YOUR LIFE BE ONE OF REGRET?

"To become the powerful being that you are you must unlearn what makes you think that you are not."

~ Dan Warburton ~

Very few entrepreneurs have the ability to sustain the level of courage and commitment required to succeed in creating their dream entrepreneur lifestyle. Even those who do, even when they accomplish what they always considered success are left with a deep emptiness, a lack of satisfaction and simply wanting more. They are left believing that *the next thing* will bring them satisfaction. I see this again and again in the people I coach.

Why is this? In the words of the great writer William James: "Most people live – whether physically, intellectually or morally – in a very restricted circle of their potential being. We all have reservoirs of life to draw upon of which we do not dream."

The truth is that unless you fully embrace the possibilities that come with being alive you will one day feel regret for not having lived your life to its full potential. This might be as someone who didn't spend enough time with your family; perhaps for not having impacted the world in the ways you could have; or as an entrepreneur who simply didn't give it their all and ended up settling for second best.

The reasons for limiting ourselves are often because of fear of *disappointing others* by possibly failing; or fearing an inability to maintain success; or fearing being perceived by others as *not good enough* for doing what makes us truly happy. Most entrepreneurs and professionals, regardless of the results they have produced, usually end up feeling some level of a lack of satisfaction with their achievements.

If you aspire to being an entrepreneur you will likely one day awaken to the truth that you have settled for an unfulfilling work position for most of your life, or that you have never got to own your own business, or travel to experience the wonders of the world, or you've never become skilled at what you truly enjoy doing.

Other entrepreneurs I've coached wished they could do more to help others, wished they could earn more money or had more time to enjoy life. Yet they often had not done anything effective about solving the causes of these unfulfilling situations. Instead, they just complained and blamed circumstances outside of themselves for why they were stuck in unsatisfying situations.

The truth is most entrepreneurs do not have the inclination to even pick up a book like this. Doing so already sets you ahead of the rest as you are studying the limitations of your mind. You are open to unlearning the destructive ways of thinking that no longer serve you and break free of your self-imposed dissatisfaction.

Most entrepreneurs are not willing to practise such introspection or ever take on practising the self-awareness required to be successful and therefore will simply end up complaining their life away until it's too late.

Sadly, few entrepreneurs will ever realise their full potential or get anywhere near realising their dream lifestyle and most will one day awaken with deep regret about all the things they could have achieved and all the great ways they could have impacted the lives of others and yet didn't.

Right now you have two choices. Either:

1. Continue to experience the same circumstances as you do now on a daily, weekly and yearly basis. Whether this be the fulfilling or unfulfilling results you are experiencing now, you will likely stay at this same level of existence as a result of your *automatic* ways of being.

Or:

2. Choose a new way of being that can enable you to access a new future; a future of new possibilities, whole new levels of wealth in every area of your life, extraordinary freedom and mastery of a lifestyle of satisfaction on a whole new level. To actually live your dream entrepreneur lifestyle.

If you chose the first option, this book is not for you and I request you give it away to someone who will appreciate it.

If you chose the second option, then read on, as this book is for you.

You need to be 100% committed to creating and making your dream lifestyle a reality, anything less than this level of commitment and your results will likely be very disappointing, mediocre or worse.

If you are committed to creating and living your dream entrepreneur lifestyle then make a silent vow right now to choose this with 100% commitment and together let's do whatever it takes to make this a reality.

WHAT IS TRANSFORMATION?

"Transformation is the process that happens when we bring awareness to an illusion that previously we were not aware of."

~ Dan Warburton ~

Transformation is *not* to change, alter or fix something. Transformation is to make something that currently exists completely disappear and then to allow something new to arise or, through willpower, create something completely new to replace it.

This process of transformation can be applied to the subconscious views you have of yourself and the world. From my life's work as a transformational coach, I've observed that applying this process is crucial to creating the dream entrepreneur lifestyle.

All the views you have created about yourself and the world around you, usually subconsciously, have given you the knowledge you need to be safe.

Views such as *I can't fly* or *fire burns me* or *unless I eat I will die* keep us all not only safe but also alive. However, from years in personal self-development and profound self-transformations, and from now having coached over 1,000 professional people, I've clearly come to see that we all also have many other subconscious views about ourselves and our world that stop us effectively creating our dream lifestyle. It's these views you must practise bringing your awareness to so you can transform them. If you don't, you will simply continue to create the same results again and again. You'll stay at your current levels of success (or lack of) and progression will likely be very, very slow.

To apply transformation effectively, you need to bring awareness to a disempowering, subconscious view (an interpretation or belief) that you have about yourself and your world. As soon as you bring awareness to a subconscious view, it's no longer subconscious. Through awareness we become conscious and as a result that view begins to lose its dominance over us. If we maintain an adequate period of awareness of the disempowering view, particularly through ongoing effective coaching dialogues, it can be vanished completely. Only then can you allow a new empowered view of yourself to arise and replace the previously disempowering view, or you can deliberately create a new and empowered view of yourself to displace the old one.

This process is *transformation*.

To transform (or unlearn) a disempowering subconscious view of yourself will always lead you to create a new view that is empowering. The reason is none of us, at the level of our true human nature, want to be trapped in suffering. Once we bring awareness to such a view (a fundamental way of thinking) that no longer serves us, naturally we don't wish to replace it with another disempowering view.

Transformation only ever has the effect of clearing away what no longer empowers us, which gives us a fresh, clear mental space to create a new view and way of being that does empower us.

Until a disempowering view that may be dominating us is cleared we cannot layer a new empowering view on top of it. For instance, we cannot behave from the view of I'm not good enough and at the same time behave from an empowering view such as I can be free. It's just not possible. The two ways of viewing ourselves and the world cause contradictory states of being. In this case we'd need to first become aware of the subconscious view of I'm not good enough, then awaken to seeing it for what it is: a false opinion of ourselves and nothing more. Only then can we let go of such a limiting view and witness it vanish. Only then can we take on a new view of ourselves such as I can be free.

This is why I don't suggest to my clients that they practise positive affirmations. I'm not saying they're not effective. In Buddhism, devotees use mantras, which are powerful sentences, to clear away ego-based shadows. However, these must be repeated many times and often for years to have a powerful mind-cleansing effect.

Instead, I suggest my clients take the route of transformation because I want them to experience much faster freedom from their past. Sometimes I'll simply request my entrepreneurial client be in action until they catch themselves procrastinating, resisting or avoiding doing something they know they need to do to truly succeed. At this stage I coach them to work out what the disempowering view is that they have which is subconsciously causing them not to undertake those important actions.

Then through transformational coaching I work with them to *vanish* the view so they can experience not being weighed down by the view any longer. Once this is done, a state of being empowered simply rises through them and their motivation to be in action again instantly returns.

The ideal is for you to undergo this process of transformation through receiving transformational coaching. If not this, though not as effective, you can practise implementing transformation through the exercise I'll guide you through later in this book.

This process of transformation you must undergo again and again until you clear the ways of thinking that no longer serve you and instead you become focused and an effective action taker. Only then will you create those profoundly fulfilling results and get to tangibly live your dream entrepreneur lifestyle.

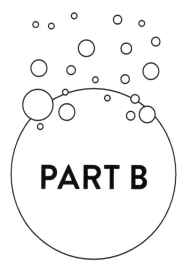

PART B

THE REFLECTION TRANSFORMATION SYSTEM™

THE REFLECTION TRANSFORMATION SYSTEM™

"You'll succeed when you unlearn the cause of what is stopping you implementing what you already know."

~ Dan Warburton ~

This system is made up of a series of exercises that to be truly effective must be carried out in writing. Don't look at this as an extra chore to everything you have going on already because implementing this system will enable you to achieve greater results with less time and effort. It's also designed so that all the areas of your life become balanced with each other and truly satisfying.

You can read this book right through then return to this chapter to implement what you learn. However, be honest with yourself.

As a busy entrepreneur or professional it's unlikely that you'll go back over this again so I suggest you take this on now as you read it for the first time. The best results were produced by clients who implemented this system, carefully following the steps and writing down the realisations they gained in real time.

Having closely observed my own journey as a business owner and entrepreneur for over 20 years as well as from having coached over 1,000 ambitious individuals, I clearly see that this system has enabled me and my clients to achieve things we never imagined we possibly could.

I have refined this system over many years into the powerful, incisive system it is today. Every professional and entrepreneur I've coached through this system who then properly embraced their transformation emerged feeling renewed or reborn. Often they'd be left feeling very empowered and completely unstoppable.

This system I call *The Reflection Transformation System.*

In chapter six I spoke of the subconscious reflection creation trap, how we all end up creating a reflection of what we think we are and are not. From my years of focused practice as a coach I've seen that for us to transform and elevate the quality of our entrepreneurial lifestyle we must transform what we think we are and are not. However, this is only part of what is required for creating and living a dream lifestyle.

The Reflection Transformation System is made up of five stages:

- Awaken Awareness

- Transformation – *The 7 Point Transformational Mandala System*

- Dream The Dream

- Choose The Dream – *The Future Focused Plan*

- Live The Dream

The system must include all five stages and must be undergone in sequence.

From my coaching experience, most entrepreneurs especially those who are currently in a challenging situation, are feeling stuck, are lacking in inspiration or are in a place of dissatisfaction must especially go through the above sequence as outlined here to ensure optimum results.

If you are currently in a generally empowered phase of your life and you are simply interested in implementing this process to succeed in a whole new way then I still suggest you also implement this system in the order as I've outlined here. Even if you are generally in a good place right now, you'll still likely be subconsciously operating at a level of performance, *a way of being* that will only enable you to continually create similar results and nothing new.

The problem for most entrepreneurs is that if you begin by *Dreaming The Dream* from where you are now you will likely end up only envisioning a future based on your current subconscious views of yourself and the world. Often this is a limited past-event-based view, which can leave you going round in circles and again merely experiencing the same results from your actions.

I remember coaching a young entrepreneur from London last year. He wanted to succeed in creating an Instagram marketing coaching business. He was working very long hours yet couldn't seem to get his business past his current earning capacity. He also dreamed of travelling and going to Japan but this never seemed possible because he found himself working such long hours all the time.

After I took him through this *reflection transformation system* he was able to clearly dream his future and become clear on what exactly he could do to help other entrepreneurs to succeed. This enabled him to set up powerful enrolment calls with potential new clients. As a result, within only three months he created a whole series of new high-ticket coaching clients. His life became much more streamlined and he told me that he's never experienced being able to earn so much money with such little effort and have so much spare time to enjoy travelling. After many years of thinking about it, he's now on holiday in Japan having the time of his life.

If you choose to properly implement *The Reflection Transformation System* then I suggest you keep a notepad and pen close to this book, or the device you are reading it on, so you can undertake each exercise in writing as outlined.

If you choose to read this book first, before participating fully in number two of *The Reflection Transformation System*, which is the transformational exercise, then this will only be effective if you commit to carrying out this exercise in full afterwards. This is the same for the other sections which all rely on each other to ensure you'll be able to generate truly extraordinary results.

Alternatively, if you choose to read this book and not implement this *reflection transformation system* or to fully participate in its written exercises then this is also acceptable; however, please know that you will only get back results that reflect the amount of energy you put into participating in this.

Remember, we all end up creating a reflection of how we *be*.

STEP 1.
AWAKEN AWARENESS

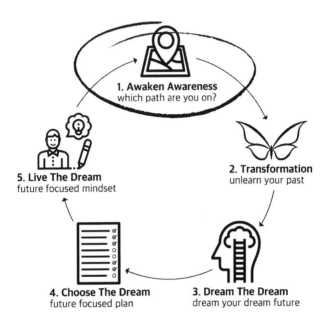

No amount, I repeat no amount of work or effort will effectively enable you to succeed at creating your dream entrepreneur lifestyle until you take 100% responsibility for the way your lifestyle is, or isn't, right now.

Until this happens you'll always have circumstances and conditions around you to blame for your current lack of satisfaction. Whether you blame a lack of jobs, that a parent was too strict, that taxes are too high, that your market is already saturated or that you don't have the required skills.

If you continue to blame circumstances around you, you will never succeed anywhere near the level you're capable of. Instead, you'll blame external circumstances and likely just give up. When it comes to creating and living the dream entrepreneur lifestyle not only is it crucial that you become 100% responsible for the way your life is and isn't now. You must also clearly distinguish the kind of future you choose as opposed to where you are presently.

Let me explain what I mean.

Imagine if one day you woke up and remembered that you were going on holiday abroad and you were to take a flight. You set off for the airport then when you arrive you realise you hadn't chosen the destination of your holiday. What would you do then? Exactly. You wouldn't know which plane to board. You'd be lost and would need to choose a destination before continuing your journey.

This is the same for your dream entrepreneur lifestyle, which is your *dream destination*. You need to have a clear idea of your dream destination otherwise you simply cannot tell if you are moving towards it or not. You can't effectively move towards a destination that is not set. It's this simple yet most professionals and entrepreneurs do not get the basic need or truth of this.

In *Dream The Dream*, the third step of the *5 step reflection transformation system*, I begin enabling you to get clear on the lifestyle you truly choose. However, initially it's highly ineffective for you to begin trying to clarify your dream destination until you distinguish where you are now in your life before setting off. To begin evaluating this, in your mind ask yourself this question:

What part of my entrepreneurial journey and lifestyle am I not entirely satisfied with?

Then once you've got this in your mind ask yourself:

What actions am I taking, or not taking, that are likely to be keeping me at the current level of success (or lack of) that I am experiencing now?

If you truly choose to create and live your dream entrepreneur lifestyle it's crucial for you to ascertain what kind of future the actions that you are currently taking (or not taking) are causing you to be headed towards. Only when this is established will you know whether to continue being the way you are now or not.

At the same time, this may be futile knowledge if you are not clear on the destination that you are headed for, but for now let's assume that you simply want to live the dream entrepreneur lifestyle and that the way you want to get there is by earning money by doing what you love.

See this path diagram:

The problem with most of the ambitious individuals I've coached is that they simply will not take responsibility for all the actions they take that are not aligned with creating their dream lifestyle. Many such committed individuals think they are on path 1, as shown in the diagram above, but the truth is they simply are not. Most and likely you are on path 2, which is completely off track.

For instance, I bet some of you check your emails or get lost in social media first thing in the morning. Or you have a to-do list but somehow always end up having to handle other more seemingly urgent matters. If not perhaps you spend hours doing something less constructive such as cleaning or daydreaming instead of writing that book you've been wanting to write. Maybe you waste time by being in conflict with colleagues. Or you let others constantly distract you from your mission.

These are just a few of the highly ineffective actions (or non-actions) you may be taking that are leaving you well off course from creating your dream lifestyle. These actions are likely not enabling you to progress towards living your dream entrepreneur lifestyle. Yet most professionals and entrepreneurs keep doing things like this and wonder why they are still not succeeding or why their dream lifestyle is taking them so much longer to create than they anticipated.

You might wake up late or have a morning routine that's not conducive to making you energetic. Instead of doing a yoga workout or going to the gym you find anything else to do but this.

Each day you may then look at a list of things you think you need to do. You then look at the list and start with the easier ones and somehow always manage to overlook those actions you know are truthfully the most important. By the end of the day you've managed to procrastinate and avoid. You are often left feeling lethargic and upon reflection the best part of the day was the lunch! But even then you didn't relax fully because you were mulling over all the important actions you should to be taking to succeed but haven't been.

This is a very common scenario with most of the entrepreneurs I coach.

Imagine that such ineffective routines, ones that don't serve you to move forwards towards your dream destination then continue for days, weeks, months and even years. Can you see what your life will look like? Can you see how you would most likely not realise your dream ambitions? Can you see how you might leave an employment position you're currently in out of frustration only to repeat the same experiences in another position in another company? Can you see that unless something radical happens to you you'd likely continually drift along as you have been even if you don't enjoy it? Or that you'll just end up with a mediocre existence and just pay rent and taxes until the day you die?

Sadly, most professionals and entrepreneurs refuse to be honest with themselves and it's only a matter of time before one day they awaken with deep regret as they realise that they have not fulfilled their life's potential. They'll feel sad and ashamed that they didn't do something truly great, that they didn't leave something inspiring for their children and that they didn't positively impact our world in a way that they could have done.

If you are feeling concern that one day this could be your life then let this land and let it land hard! I say this to you not only because this is likely your truth but because unless you become aware of this you won't do anything differently and that future you fear will almost certainly become a reality.

Alternatively, the actions that are likely to enable you to create your dream lifestyle are actions like exercise during early morning, delegating your smaller admin jobs, making requests of others to support you and your vision, unsubscribing from every email subscription that is wasting your time, following a plan based on exactly the future you choose and then to only take the actions in that plan. Other actions that will likely get you to the next level are to pick up the phone and create sales or to schedule powerful meetings with people that can make all the difference to your success.

Though this is obvious why do so many ambitious individuals fail to take such actions? Why do they waste so much time?

Take your pen and begin by writing the answer to these questions:

- What things can you see that you do that are wasting your time and are not effectively enabling you to move towards you living your dream lifestyle?

- If you continue taking (or not taking) these actions what is the future that you are likely headed for?

- If you continue doing these ineffective things what will your life likely look like in ten years from today?

Take a break from reading and come back when you've written down at least five sentences.

If you apply these questions effectively, you'll see that whatever the lifestyle you are experiencing now, in years to come you'll likely end up in the same kind of situations and with the same kind of results.

How can I confidently state this?

It's simple. All of your past actions and ways of being have been what has caused you to create and live the lifestyle that you are experiencing now. Unless you change how you are being and the actions you regularly take, it's highly likely that not much will change. You'll just find yourself back to where you are now but simply older, more tired and even more dissatisfied with these areas of your life that you'd love to be different.

With this in mind begin by awakening your awareness, become 100% responsible for your lifestyle as it is now, and become aware of the actions that are ineffective and the future you are likely headed for.

Until you get the severity of this, you won't do anything differently and that future you don't want will become your reality.

STEP 2.
TRANSFORMATION

The 7 Point Transformational Mandala System

It is only when you transform the thought-based causes of your ineffective actions (or lack of taking effective actions) that you will then be able to free yourself of ineffective behavioural patterns (ways of being that no longer serve you). If you manage to do this you'll find it much easier to take new and effective actions that will enable you to access a completely new and inspirational future.

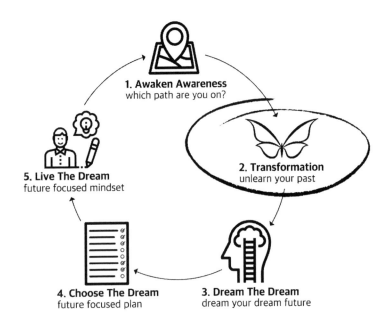

1. **Awaken Awareness**
which path are you on?

2. **Transformation**
unlearn your past

3. **Dream The Dream**
dream your dream future

4. **Choose The Dream**
future focused plan

5. **Live The Dream**
future focused mindset

In this section I'm going to break down my *7 Point Transformational Mandala System*. It is a seven-point coaching conversational journey that I've taken nearly all my one-to-one clients through. It's taken me over 15 years of focused personal self-development and over eight years of intensely coaching others to be able to create and arrive at this refined transformational coaching system.

This system enables the recipient to unlearn the main disempowering views they subconsciously have of themselves and the world that have been holding them back from performing at the level they need to sustain to truly succeed as an entrepreneur.

This is the *7 Point Transformational Mandala System*.

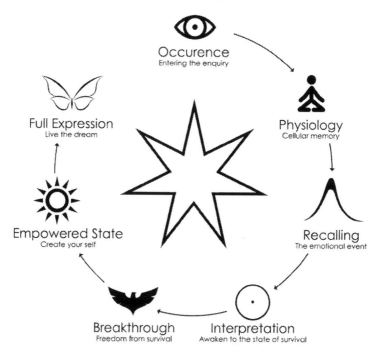

If you would like to experience this transformational process effectively then there is no better way than to be guided in a coaching conversation with me. If you'd like this please feel free to contact me. My contact details are at the end of this book.

Alternatively, I'll break this down so you can go through the process and implement it yourself. Though it won't be as profound, it can still be highly effective and lead you to a life-transforming breakthrough. You will require at least one hour of uninterrupted time, a pen and some writing paper.

As we get to each section simply write the title of each section then answer the questions as outlined. To undertake this exercise properly turn off all your other distractions and do not eat while undergoing the process. If you let yourself get distracted, or indulge yourself in food or anything else, you'll avoid the breakthrough available to you. Just trust me on this.

To go through this process successfully on your own is going to take courage and extra focus.

Ensure that you are able to complete this entire section in one go and allow up to two hours in case you commence some deep transformational revelations that require sustained focus to complete.

If you don't have the time for this now put this book down and schedule a better time as it will not be as effective to stop and start while amidst this process. Do this properly or don't do it all.

If you are ready, let's get to work!

1. Occurrence

To enter into this process begin by writing the title *Occurrence* at the top of a new page and be prepared to take down a short bullet list of notes.

Everyone has a different occurrence of the world, of life, of themselves and of others. The way these things occur to me is different from how they occur to you. Any human experience of something, or occurrence of something, is neither right nor wrong, it is purely an occurrence of the way something is and isn't for you, me or for any other individual.

Begin by being honest with yourself:

Which area of your lifestyle isn't the way you want it to be right now and would like to elevate?

As a professional or entrepreneur you might be wondering why I am not guiding you to only look at your business results, right? Well, I've discovered that everything in our lives is closely connected together. If you cause a transformation in your experiences of relationships or in your experience of health you will actually also have a transformational effect on your abilities to create your dream lifestyle. If you are truly committed to succeed in an extraordinary way then trust me on this and go with this process as I outline for you here.

There is always at least one area of our life that we wish to elevate because it is human nature to always want to improve and grow. If you don't have an area of your life you'd like to elevate then I request you look more deeply. It's likely you are avoiding being honest with yourself. I strongly doubt you would be reading a book on self-transformation if everything was already amazing for you.

The area of your life you may wish to improve could be business, your work, lifestyle, relationships, finances, health or any other area you are dissatisfied with and wanting to improve. This may also be an area of your life that's been unsatisfying for a while but you've avoided admitting it.

As you become aware of this area of your life, answer this question:

What if nothing changed? How do I feel about this area of my life always being the same as it is now?

Begin to write down what comes to you, however your answers need only be short and things like annoyed, depressed, resigned, frustrated or angry.

The skill here is to be totally honest with yourself. If you begin to feel emotion then this is a really good sign you are effectively entering into this enquiry. Just trust this process and write down a list of how the thought of this area of your life never improving or changing makes you feel.

Alternatively, if you really can't see an area of your life you'd like to improve then ask yourself these questions:

- How do I feel when things don't go to plan or take much longer than planned?

- How do I feel when someone is late for a meeting and doesn't communicate?

- How do I feel when I'm not paid on time or when I don't have enough money?

Answering these questions will enable you to effectively enter into this enquiry as long as the answers are not like: I just move on, I get very focused or I just find a solution. These answers are simply reactive and not truthful. Instead, be honest with yourself and write down how these circumstances cause you to truly feel whenever you are faced with them.

2. Physiology

Start a new section by writing the title *Physiology* on a new page.

The more I coach people the more I realise that there is more memory in our body than there is in our brain! The physical sensations in our bodies are the keys to us becoming aware of memories we've forgotten. Science has now begun to prove that our cells communicate with each other so it makes sense that our physical sensations (and feelings) are able to trigger us to remember subconscious memories in our brain.

In this section write down the answer to this question:

Where in my body do I feel the sensations (or feelings) I wrote down?

And:

What is that feeling like?

For this section you simply need to bring your awareness to those physical feelings.

My clients find themselves writing descriptions like a tightness in my chest and shallow breathing or heavy in my body or fizzing in my hands or hot around my head or a knot in my stomach.

If you can't describe the sensation then simply write *a sensation in my chest* or wherever you feel associated sensations. The objective is to become aware of how you physically sense the descriptive words you wrote in the previous section.

If these sensations seem familiar, or you often feel these feelings or feel them all the time then this is a great indication that you are on track to gaining an amazing insight.

3. Recalling

Begin by writing down *Recalling* as a new section.

By now you should have become aware of how the world occurs for you when things don't go to plan or when you imagine this area of your life always being the same as it is now.

Next you wrote a short bullet list of *occurrences* (or feelings).

Then for the second part of these seven steps you have written down how you physically feel these feelings.

In this section, answer this question:

When was the first time I ever felt these physical sensations?

Initially, I know you'll be thinking that there is no way you can remember this. From my coaching experience this is normal. Every time you think this, come back to the question:

When was the first time I ever felt these physical sensations?

You wouldn't believe how many times I hear people say they can't remember anything and then they start to uncover a memory. Trust me, your brain has recorded your whole life in detail.

Keep coming back to this question:

When was the first time I ever felt these physical sensations?

At some point you will remember something that happened. The younger you were when this happened, the greater the transformation you'll gain from this. If two different events come to mind, just go with the event that happened when you were the most young.

You are looking for a moment in your past that was challenging for you in some way. Maybe you were shouted at, maybe you became embarrassed at school or you were bullied. Maybe a brother or sister did something to you or maybe you were totally alone when something frightening happened. Maybe you've experienced something quite traumatic. If this is the case then this is your opportunity to heal yourself of that event and free yourself of the associated pain.

As I said, this is going to take focus and courage.

When recalling an event, if you didn't feel exactly the same feelings back then as you wrote down in step 2, don't worry, just enter the enquiry through feeling these feelings initially then flow with the memory that arises.

As you remember an event, write it down as if it was happening now by completing these sentences:

- I am... years old

- I am standing or sitting in the... (living room or on the playground)

- I am with my... (teacher, mum, dad, brother, sister, friend or neighbour)

- What was said was...

- What I said is...

- Or what happened was...

You only need a few short sentences to effectively recall the event. If you are feeling emotional then simply pause, allow yourself to feel what you feel then continue. There is no right or wrong way you should or shouldn't feel right now. Just allow this process to flow and complete all seven steps to ensure you properly free yourself of the repercussions of this past-based event. For this section there is nothing more you need to do other than just allow yourself to remember an event somehow associated with the sensations (or feelings) you wrote in the previous section and a few details to describe what happened.

4. Interpretation

Begin by writing *Interpretation* at the start of a new section on a new page.

Completing this section with care is vital if you wish to carry out this transformational process effectively. As you bring your awareness to the memory of this event that was challenging or difficult for you, answer this question:

What was I thinking at the time?

Starting with *I am... or I am not...*

The answer you are *not* looking for is *I am not able to do this* or *I am confused* but rather you are looking for a description of yourself. Look deeper.

From my experience as a coach, the events we found challenging and difficult usually have the experience of happening to us. Meaning that we couldn't control what was happening.

So a good place to start is to bring yourself back to the memory of the event (as if it was happening again now).

Complete either of these sentences:

I cannot control what is happening because I am...

Or: *Because I am not...*

Right now you might be feeling hungry, or not wanting to continue with this process. This is normal. Just be with these sensations and remain focused, as the rewards of completing this properly will be extraordinary for you.

What you are looking for is a disempowering interpretation that you invented about yourself during this challenging moment.

These are some of the interpretations my clients made during such past events that they remembered experiencing:

- I'm not good enough

- I'm not loved

- I'm not wanted

- I'm not in control

- I'm not safe

- I'm not clever

- I don't fit in

- I'm different

- I'm alone

- I'm small

- I'm weak

- I'm not noticed

- I'm invisible

- I'm wrong

- I'm stupid

- I don't belong here

Use this list purely as a guide as it's important for you to find your own disempowering interpretation (or view) that you invented during your past event. Equally you may find that one of these interpretations (or views) really resonates with you emotionally and if one feels as so, just write it down.

Take your time and if you come up with something like *I can't do this...* then again ask yourself *why?* The answer will always come to you when you ask yourself: *Because I am not... or I am...*

If you can ask yourself and answer these questions effectively then you'll highly likely become aware of something that will change (transform) your life forever.

Once you have written down your disempowering interpretation see if there is a second part to it. Through leading coaching sessions and for me personally I've found there is often a second interpretation or view linked to the first.

For instance, one of my disempowering interpretations is *I'm not good enough* and the second part is *nobody wants me.*

Here is the same list with the possible second part added:

- I'm not good enough, I'm stupid

- I'm not loved, nobody wants me

- I'm not wanted, I'm ugly

- I'm not in control, I'm weak

- I'm not safe, I'm small

- I'm not clever, I'm stupid

- I don't fit in, I'm ugly

- I'm different, nobody loves me

- I'm alone, I'm not safe

- I'm small, I'm weak

- I'm weak, I'm not strong

- I'm not noticed, I'm not good enough

- I'm invisible, I don't matter

- I'm wrong, I'm not clever

- I'm stupid, nobody wants me

- I'm ugly, nobody cares

- I don't belong here, I'm different

Once you've got something like this written down, trust you've got it right and continue. Don't overthink this, simply trust this process.

As you read over what you've written you might be thinking was I really thinking this, or *no,* that can't be right. Ignore such thoughts. This is you trying to intellectualise your experience. It's likely the survival part of your brain is simply not wanting you to admit to what you are uncovering.

I want you to go beyond your intellectual mind and instead simply find the courage to admit that you could well have been thinking something like this at the time of this event you have remembered.

Well done for completing this section. This takes a lot of focus and courage.

5. Breakthrough

So far we have been using feelings to guide you. You've enquired about how you would feel if the area of your life that isn't as you'd like it was to be continued. Or how you feel when things don't go to plan or when you don't have enough money.

Then I asked you to describe how you physically feel these sensations. I then guided you to feel these feelings and as you did so to recall the event where you first remembered feeling these or similar sensations and feelings.

At this stage, while recalling the event associated with those feelings I asked you what were you thinking as this event happened starting with *I'm...* and *I'm not...* All of this was based on you utilising your feelings to access what previously was a distant and forgotten memory.

In this section we are going to move from focusing on your *feelings* to focusing on *being.* The realm of being is something that is primarily only a human phenomenon. It encompasses everything to do with you speaking, communicating, moving, taking action and doing. All this is the being part of being human and means behaviour.

Focusing on *being* during these remaining sections will enable you to gain a new transformational insight and access a completely new future. From now on you'll be enquiring into how you've been *being* – your disempowering interpretation (or view) and the effects this has had on your ability to succeed. This will become clearer as I guide you through this section.

If you don't do this section of this process properly, transformation will not be possible. You can't transform or unlearn a way of being that you are not aware of. So, this section is aimed at enabling you to do exactly that: to become clearly aware of this past-based way of *being* and how it has been holding you back.

To begin, write down the title of this section, *Breakthrough*.

Next, write the subtitle, *Unwanted Impacts*.

Now write this question:

What are the unwanted impacts that I have in my life as a result of me being (insert your disempowering interpretation here)?

Your question should read something like this:

What are the unwanted impacts that I have in my life as result of me being 'I'm not good enough, nobody wants me'?

Or:

What are the unwanted impacts that I have in my life as result of being 'I'm not clever, I'm stupid'?

Or:

What are the unwanted impacts that I have in my life as result of me being 'I'm not safe, I'm alone'?

As you write this question down begin reflecting on what the answers might be. If you are still unclear, then think about this.

What are the things you have in your life that you don't want to have in your life as a result of *being* this way? Or: what is it that you avoid doing when you feel like you really are your disempowering interpretation? For instance, when you might feel something like *I'm not good enough* or *I'm not clever enough* or *I'm a failure?*

When you really feel like you are these ways, are you social or do you spend more time alone? Are you jumping with joy? Likely not.

So what do you do instead?

While you feel you really are your interpretation, what is it you don't do that you know you need to do? Do you perhaps not express yourself? Do you avoid selling yourself? Do you overeat, watch hours of online films or waste hours browsing social media?

Maybe you avoid talking to your boss? Maybe you avoid asking for a pay rise? Maybe you often say yes to requests others make of you that you are really not interested in doing? Maybe you do whatever it takes to please others and neglect things you want to do? Maybe you keep wasting your money and not investing in yourself?

Have a look, keep reflecting, keep looking at this and do not let your ego, which does not want you to take responsibility for this, distract you. Keep coming back to this enquiry and don't stop until you have at least ten items written down.

As you begin writing a list of unwanted impacts ask yourself: What is the unwanted impact of me doing this? And what is the unwanted result I am left with because of me doing this?

Now close this book and keep writing until you can't think of anything more.

Once you have a list of at least ten items, if you have done this correctly you should be feeling confronted and shocked at what you've written. You should be starting to become aware of how damaging this way of being is on you and your abilities of creating your dream lifestyle.

If I was to go through this same process for my own primary disempowering interpretation of *I'm not good enough nobody wants me* I'd write something like this:

- I work long hours and burn myself out trying to prove I am good enough

- No matter what results I get, I am left feeling like what I've done is not good enough

- I don't feel like continuing to work because whatever I do it never seems enough

- I avoid introducing myself and what I do

- I avoid selling myself

- I argue and always try to be right

- I don't listen to others

- I don't make sales

- I am left ashamed that I'm failing and not succeeding

- I always pretend that everything is ok and secretly hide that I'm failing

- I don't have enough money to do what I want

- I'm not impacting the world as I could

- I am of no use to humanity

- I am letting my partner and family down

- I feel sad that I'm not getting any decent results and that I'm failing

- I feel like I'll never succeed and that I'll always be a failure

Clearly, you **must** be as honest with yourself as I have been with myself here. If you don't become as honest with yourself you will not transform anything and you will continue at your current level of lack of success. I know that this self-honesty isn't easy but if you truly want to succeed you must practise being so.

Stay with this process and keep going until you've written down a whole series of unwanted impacts that start to leave you feeling heavy and likely rather sad.

Now write down and answer this question:

What will my life look like in ten years if I continue to be this way?

Be totally honest with yourself.

Look carefully at the unwanted impacts you've written down. Look at the unwanted results the associated ineffective actions leave you with. Can you see how damaging you being this way is on your life? Do you get a sense that being this way for another ten years will just leave you ending up with the same results as you have now and nothing more... or even worse? Can you see that nothing will particularly change, that nothing new will be created and that you'll be in the same situation yet simply so many more years older?

You must allow yourself to feel emotionally impacted by this. Unless you allow yourself to fully feel this you'll just go back to that likely and predictable future, so do this work properly and stay with this. You are doing really well, this transformational work is not easy.

Can you see how actually there is no way you'll ever be able to create and live your dream lifestyle with this way of being dominating you and your actions? Can you see how this way of being is the very thing that is leaving you headed for a future where at some point you'll wake up with deep regret? Can you see how this way of being just does not serve you at all any longer?

By now you should have become aware of how being this way is actually ruining your life and be feeling emotional about this. If you are not, then you are avoiding doing this deeper inner work and I suggest you go back over it again before continuing.

For you who is feeling the emotional impact of this, write down these questions:

Do I get how destructive this way of being is on me and my life?

And write this question down:

Do I see how this way of being will cause me to never be able to succeed to the level that I could?

Also write this question down:

Do I see how this way of being does not serve me any longer?

The answer to these three questions should be a clear *yes*.

So, go ahead and reply to each of these questions as so.

As you go through this part of the process you might be thinking this can't be true or this is a bit overdramatic. That's ok.

I encourage you to simply trust that you are awakening to something that was previously hidden for you, that what you are starting to see really is so. Trust this process and keep going as it will all make sense. Trust me.

To conclude this section called breakthrough I have three final and very, very vital questions that you must write down, study and reply to carefully for you to get the full benefit of this deeper inner work and gain a rewarding self-transformation.

Skipping this or answering these three questions ineffectively will cause all the work you've done so far to be useless. So pay close attention and stay focused.

Here is the first of three final questions. Write this down:

Who invented this way of being?

Think about it. Did you ever see any of these or something like any of these statements ever written on a wall?

- I'm not good enough, I'm stupid

- I'm not loved, nobody wants me

- I'm not wanted, I'm ugly

- I'm not in control, I'm weak

- I'm not safe, I'm small

- I'm not clever, I'm stupid

- I don't fit in, I'm ugly

- I'm different, nobody loves me

- I'm alone, I'm not safe

- I'm small, I'm weak

- I'm weak, I'm not strong

- I'm not noticed, I'm not good enough

- I'm invisible, I don't matter

- I'm wrong, I'm not clever

- I'm stupid, nobody wants me

- I'm ugly, nobody cares

- I don't belong here, I'm different

Were any of these statements or something similar written on a giant banner being pulled by an airplane as it flew past? I'm sure it wasn't.

Were you specifically told that you were this disempowering way of being?

The answer to this question is *no*. So, go ahead and write this answer down exactly:

I invented this.

That's it. Nothing more. Just write that down, trust me and trust yourself.

If you are keeping up with this then well done.

Now write down this second to last question:

Is this way of being true?

Well is it? If you invented it, is it true? Have a look at this. Who invented the meanings of every word in that sentence that describes your disempowering interpretation (or way of being)? For instance, if we look at I'm not good enough. What does good actually mean?

If I was to ask 100 people what good is I'm sure I'd get 100 different definitions. Think about it. The meaning you have given to each word is your own invented meaning and no one else's view.

Added to this, let's look at the *I am* or *I'm* in the sentence.

Where is *I* or *you*? Point at where you think you are right now? Are you in your chest or are you in your head? If I cut your body open I'll find *you*, will I? Really? No, of course I won't. The concept of *I* is an ego construct made up of all the things you think you are and are not.

And I'm not speaking about your body either. Your body is however your body is, and isn't. Your body has both its capabilities and in-capabilities. I am asking *you* the thing, the essence, the being that is expressed through the body you currently have. That intangible thing we call *you*. Can it be described (labelled) as this way of being? No it can't, it can't be true.

An object like a chair is a solid object that we can see. I can describe it as being red in colour or heavy in weight because it's tangible yet you as in I is not tangible at all.

You cannot be labelled with any kind of definitive or descriptive label. Get it?

If you happen to have distinguished an interpretation of *I'm not in control* then I ask you what do you think you are in control of exactly? If someone asks you *Can we meet at 9am tomorrow?* then you reply *Yes I can, I promise to be there.* Can you really promise this? You cannot because you really never know for sure that you won't get hit by a bus before then or that a terrorist bomb won't go off near the person where you were meant to meet. I don't mean to be gruesome here, I'm just using these scenarios to guide you to understand that you can't promise anything so do you have control over what can happen?

The truth is, you can't.

You can do many things to ensure such events are unlikely to happen and to increase your safety, however you can never be certain. Why? Because in truth you know you don't have control over anything. So, if you've written *I'm not in control* and can now see you don't have control over anything, how can *I'm not in control* be true, now that you know that you can't be in control of anything to begin with?

It doesn't make sense, because it's simply not true. The only thing we actually have control over is how we respond to situations, which I'll cover later in this chapter.

Maybe you wrote down something like *I'm not clever enough.* So, let's look at this one.

What does *clever enough* actually mean?

There was a time when you couldn't tie your shoelaces, right? Or you couldn't write your own name, right? Well, during those times in your life were you really *not clever enough?* Or were these simply skills you hadn't yet learned? I agree that at these early stages in your life these were things that you were unable to do. However, to give such a definite description of yourself, a totally intangible entity as *not clever enough* as if you are a fixed object just doesn't make sense.

Furthermore, looking at this possible disempowering interpretation, who says you are *not clever enough?* And compared to what or who?

You may not be able to do something yet but with practice, in most cases, you can learn. Of course, you may have a physical impediment that stops you being able to do that physical action. I'm not disputing this. But are you your body? No you are not. You are some energy, some expressive entity, some human being phenomenon that is simply expressing itself through the use of your body. Makes sense, doesn't it?

So, let's refer to this thing or energy that we call *you.*

Is it a fixed object? Can you point it out without the use of your body? No, you cannot so how can any description such as *I'm not clever enough, I don't belong, I'm different* or *I'm not good enough* be true if you don't even have something tangible in the first place that can be described as so? Exactly, you can't. Therefore, whatever disempowering interpretation (of way of being) you've invented, the answer to this question is:

This is not true.

Go ahead and write down this answer to this second last question. Now take a deep breath in, and out.

Well done for getting this far. This is not a straightforward or easy conversation. This takes courage and focus and you are doing really, really well.

Here is the final question. Write this down:

Do I need to be this way any longer?

Do you? Do you actually need to be this way any longer?

If you recall that challenging moment, when that difficult event happened, the survival part of your brain had to make sense of it because you needed to understand what actions were needed to survive what happened. In that past moment, in that difficult event that was out of your control, the survival part of your brain interpreted how the world occurred with a sentence that started off with *I'm not... I'm...*

The problem is that this happened subconsciously and then ever since remained as so − a subconscious interpretation (or view) of yourself and the world. That event is not happening any longer is it? That unique moment with its circumstances has passed, am I right?

So, do you need to be this way any longer?

No you don't. Why? Because it was just an interpretation, a fictitious invention *you made up* about who you thought you were in that moment.

And that moment has now passed.

If you are carrying out this deeper inner work effectively then you might be facing a challenge from the part of your brain that handles your survival processes. This part of your brain is likely trying to convince you that the insights you are having are not true and that you cannot stop being this way. The survival part of your brain knows no other way than to continue being this way.

Why is this?

This is because this part of your brain that is obsessive about your survival doesn't want you to become aware of this lack of truth because it believes it has used this way of being to get everything it has needed up until now *including* love, attention, acceptance, money, the relationships you have now and even the success you've had so far.

This is a highly damaging illusion that you must awaken out of. If you don't, you will continue being as you've always been being before because you are subconsciously thinking that you need to continue being so to continue getting these same things you've got before, when in truth you don't. It's this past way of being that has caused you to continually create the dissatisfying things and entrepreneurial results you have now.

Even if these results are good, they will remain the kind of results you'll keep producing and **nothing** more. You'll be stuck at whatever level of performance you're at now.

The problem is, this disempowering interpretation of yourself has become a *default survival state.*

It's become an automatic way of being (or reacting) that you have adopted and continue to express regardless of the situation you are in. It's like using a big and heavy sledgehammer for every job. This big and heavy sledgehammer might work well for knocking down a brick wall but will not work well for hammering tiny little carpentry nails into wood. We need another kind of hammer for this application and this is the same as for ways of being. One way of being is required to get one result out of one situation and another way of being is required to get another result out of another situation.

Mastery of the self is being able to be as you choose to be in every situation to gain the result you choose out of every situation.

The problem for most professionals and entrepreneurs is that your default survival state (your disempowering interpretation) is set to automatic to survive every moment, leaving you reacting ineffectively to each moment.

It might work to get a few results you want in some areas of life, but not in all.

If you want to effectively lead a team and you're dealing with a challenged employee, you are better to stop and listen with compassion before you can answer wisely and lead them to find a solution.

If you want to create a fulfilling work environment and someone confronts you at work over a mistake you've made, you need to understand their viewpoint before skilfully responding. If you want to start a business successfully you may need to continually carry out sales calls, knock on many doors or get up on stage and be powerfully expressive.

The problem is your default survival state (your disempowering interpretation) dominates you all the time and in every area of your life – especially under pressure.

Yes, it may be useful at times and yes it could well be what has enabled you to succeed to the levels that you have now, but after a while it becomes the very thing that holds you back from progressing and properly succeeding.

When you are dominated by such an interpretation or view of the world you don't have other modes of self-expression, or you have an inability to be tactile or loving when required. Instead you just react in an attempt to prove to everyone that you are not what you subconsciously fear you are. You react in an attempt to prove that you are good enough or that you are loveable or that you are not weak. This is usually experienced by others as defensive, aggressive, dismissive, unloving or even violent.

Maybe whatever your boss, your partner or parents say to you, you react in the same way every time? Maybe whenever you think about money, or have to deal with money, you feel the same physical reactions? Maybe when you get the chance to speak to someone important you automatically feel the same sensations and then react in the same manner?

If any of this is so, then these are moments in your life where you are finding yourself being dominated by this subconscious and disempowering interpretation of yourself and the world.

The problem is that this way of viewing yourself and the world doesn't just dominate you when you are amidst events that cause you to feel challenged, but it will actually be subconsciously causing you to avoid situations where you may feel these unwanted feelings again. You'll be avoiding meeting important people, you'll be avoiding making sales calls, you'll be avoiding taking on an opportunity to speak on stage, and you'll likely avoid taking actions that could cause you to fail, which are probably the actions you need to take to succeed!

So, you play small and generally avoid anything that might cause change in your life. Why? Because you fear that if you fail everyone might discover that you really are the defective thing you've been subconsciously thinking you are.

As a result you'll just keep going round in circles, you'll keep doing the things you've been doing all along and you'll experience the same kind of results again, and again, and again.

It's a vicious circle that destroys all abilities to truly succeed.

So, here are the three final questions to answer in this section:

Who invented this?

Answer with: *I invented this.*

Is it true?

Answer with: *This is not true.*

Do I need to be this way any longer?

Answer this with: *I no longer need to be this way.*

Let yourself awaken to the madness you've been living in.

Realise that *you* invented this, that it is *not* true and that you *no longer* need to be this way.

Now take a deep breath in, and out. Now let this realisation land.

If you have effectively gone through this process at this stage you'll now be left with a sense of ease, release and relief. Alternatively, if you've undergone this process effectively you may be left with a compelling question of *now what?* as you realise that your whole life up until today was dominated by surviving this way of thinking that was previously subconscious.

Either of these states of mind are positive.

They indicate you are now ready to allow (or consciously create) a new way of being to displace the old and once tiring way of being.

6. Empowered State

So far we have done the deeper work to unlearn and clear a disempowering way of viewing yourself and the world that no longer serves you. The reason I've taken you through this initial process is because it's simply not possible to be empowered if you are thinking in ways that cause you to feel disempowered.

It's not possible to be free when you are dominated by an interpretation of yourself such as I'm weak, I don't belong here or I'm not good enough.

Some people can simply let go of the past and focus on what serves them. However, from having coached entrepreneurs for many years now I've come to see that most need to first unlearn what is subconsciously causing them to avoid taking important actions before moving forward in an empowered way.

I once coached a bright lady from Singapore. She was always well dressed and had long black hair. She was a highly committed entrepreneur who had launched a business that specialised in providing security systems for business computer networks. She wasn't succeeding anywhere near to the level that I could clearly sense she could. At the time there was one thing above all that would enable her to take her business and lifestyle to the next level: it was to invite companies to big, classy boardroom meetings and to present to them what her business does. But she never found the courage to fulfil such an opportunity. She'd even had someone else offer to arrange a small gathering on her behalf but she kept turning it down out of a deep fear of public speaking.

Then during our first coaching conversation she distinguished something that happened to her when she was at school when her classmates laughed at her when she answered a teacher's question incorrectly. She saw how during that event she had interpreted herself as *I am incapable, I'm not important.* This caused her to always feel like *no one would take her seriously.* She saw that ever since this event at school she was left feeling so fearful of speaking in front of others that she always avoided doing so.

One month after this initial transformational coaching session, she called to thank me and explained that she'd taken an opportunity to speak on stage at a large event in Singapore.

She told me how she felt so much calmer than before and was able to effectively communicate the solutions her business provides to the audience members and as a result closed some sizeable deals with some of the audience members.

She has now presented at more events and as a result her business is growing faster than ever before. She'd moved her mindset from one of surviving to one of creating, but she was only able to do this once she had unlearned the ways of viewing herself that previously caused her to avoid speaking in front of audiences.

As with my Singaporean client and with most entrepreneurs, it's likely that you also often procrastinate and avoid taking those important actions then fall into unfulfilling and repetitive routines. All these are signs of surviving and not creating and the latter is what we are going to enable you to clearly define and start to operate from in this section.

Now you are going to create who you are as a way of being to totally displace that old and unfulfilling way of being.

Begin by writing and completing this statement:

Now that I no longer need to be (enter your disempowering interpretation here), *now I can be* (enter here some words that leave you feeling empowered).

The mistake to avoid is to simply write the opposite of your disempowering interpretation.

For example, if you wrote *I'm not good enough* don't simply write *Now I can be good enough* because this is enforcing *I'm not good enough.*

This is often what my clients say at this stage during this process. We then often have a coaching conversation that goes like this:

I ask them, "Who invented *I'm not good enough?* " They reply, "I did." So, I ask, "Ok, is *I'm not good enough* true?" They then reply, "No, this is not true."

I then ask, "So how can you be the opposite of something that doesn't exist?"

At this stage they usually go quiet and then they realise that it's not possible to be an opposing way of being to a way of being (and thinking) that doesn't exist. In fact, when we do this, we are simply enforcing the disempowering interpretation, we are giving it more power over us by declaring that we need to be its opposite.

Why would we do this?

Because we still subconsciously believe that this disempowered view of ourselves really is who we are.

So, be aware of not making this mistake. If you catch yourself doing this simply acknowledge that this is just you being that old way of being again, realise that you invented it, that it is not true and that you no longer need to be that way any longer.

Now come back to completing this statement again.

Now that I no longer need to be (enter your disempowering interpretation here*), now I can be* (enter here some words that leave you feeling empowered).

When I lead my clients through this part of the conversation many of them find themselves with a blank mind and are left unable to think. So I ask them, "Now that you no longer need to be this way, how do you feel?" Many reply with, "I feel good" or "I feel so much more relaxed" and then I might ask, "If you were feeling this way when walking into an important meeting how would you be being?"

Bit by bit my client starts to describe the way of feeling in such a way that they realise this is also a way of being.

To help you with this, choose three of these words that best resonate with how you feel (or can be) now:

- Alive

- Free

- Unstoppable

- Loving

- Powerful

- Omnipotent

- Liberated

- Vital

- Gentle

- Peaceful

- At ease

- Sharp

- Awake

- Grounded

- Aligned

- Present

- Flowing

- Connected

- Fully expressed

- Kind

- Centred

- Tranquil

- Light

- Expansive

Remember, you are not looking for an opposing way of being to the old survival way of being (the disempowering interpretation you distinguished) because this isn't true to begin with.

Instead you are looking for a totally new way of being that you can start to be. Just one of these states can leave us feeling totally empowered. At the same time three of these ways of being when used together in one sentence can sound and make you feel amazing.

They may read as so:

- Now I can be powerful, free and alive

- Now I can be at ease, liberated and unstoppable

- Now I can be present, loving and omnipotent

- Now I can be centred, present and expansive

- Now I can be flowing, light and grounded

Choose the three words from this list that light you up the most or choose your own words. Simply make sure that these words describe ways of being that leave you feeling a deep sense of peacefulness or that leave you feeling totally empowered!

Next, write down your new and empowered way of being and read it out loud to yourself.

If you've done this part effectively you'll find yourself feeling very much inspired as you say this out loud. If on the other hand you are not able to feel the inspiration then you are likely still in a state of survival, and I suggest going back to the start of this section or finding a skilled coach to work with to guide you through this and break through what may be holding you back.

The reason I've suggested you write your new way of being in a sentence that starts with *Now I can be* is because this gives you the freedom to be able to choose this way of being whenever you want. If this sentence was to read *Now I am* then it would be a fixed way of being regardless of the circumstances, which is constricting.

Remember that if you *be* the same way in every situation this becomes an automatic and reactionary way of *being*. So, in saying *I can be* gives you the freedom to choose to be empowered or not as you please. More importantly, this also gives you the opportunity to start *being* however is best suited for you to be, to create the results you dream of.

Rather than to react, this new ability to turn on or off an empowered state of *being* is to be able to respond. This is to have *response-ability*, which is where you become the master of choosing your response to each situation or challenge.

In the past when you were in a difficult situation you had no choice but to react as you attempted to survive an experience of the world as *I'm not loved, I don't fit in* or *I'm not wanted*.

Now you have a choice. Now you can choose how to respond to each situation.

Start by practising choosing how you respond and being this new and empowered way of being in every moment you see as suitable.

The more you practise this, the more unstoppable you'll become.

If you've completed this section effectively you will now be left feeling inspired.

If so, congratulations, you now have a new way of being, a heightened level of *response-ability* and power.

7. Full Expression

Again, congratulations for having stayed with this process. It isn't easy and really does take courage. If you are not feeling empowered or feel you are not getting anything beneficial from this then again I suggest you start this seven-point transformational process again or find a skilled coach who can effectively guide you through it.

Alternatively, if you are feeling free, empowered or peaceful (or maybe all three!) then I am so inspired at the new future that is becoming possible for you. If you feel any of these amazing feelings then please understand that although this is good, it is only an insight. This insight only becomes a breakthrough when you go out into the world, be this new way of being and take new actions that cause you to achieve results that occur to you as miraculous.

These miraculous results could be your colleagues or family members communicating back to you in a refreshing way, achieving measurable effectiveness in closing sales, or in reaching a powerful outcome in a meeting. Until anything new happens as a result of this insight it will never be a breakthrough and will only ever remain as an insight.

As you go through this final section of the *7 Point Transformational Mandala System* you should start to think of new actions you can take. In taking these actions (inspired and fuelled by this new way of being) you'll soon create new results and this insight will then become a breakthrough. For this to happen you need to start being your empowered state in your workplace, with your colleagues, with the ones you love and when you see you can be effective in any future situation or challenge you face.

This will all become clearer as you complete this written process.

To begin this final section start with writing the title *Full Expression* on a new page.

Now that you don't need to be that old and ineffective way of being any longer and instead you can be this new and empowered way of being, if you took this on, what becomes possible for you?

As you allow yourself to become inspired by the possibilities you begin to imagine, write this question:

If I chose to be (enter your three most empowering ways of being here) *what would become possible for me and my life?*

So your question may read as so:

If I chose to be alive, unstoppable and free what would become possible for me and my life?

Then begin to write everything that comes to you. For example:

- If you chose to be this way in your next meeting, what could the outcome be?

- If you chose to be this way on stage to showcase who you are and what you do then pitch a service or a product, what could become possible?

- If you chose to be this way with the people you love, with your neighbours, colleagues at work and with everyone new you met, what could become possible?

- If you chose to be this way in the face of your every challenge, what could become possible?

As you begin writing all the inspiring things that come to you, ask: *What does that make possible?* Then again... *and what does that make possible?* And again... Keep doing so until you stop finding ideas to write down.

Add to this what becomes possible for your partner? For your children? For your whole family? For the people in your country? Or even what becomes possible for the world and the whole of humanity?

- Are you getting the incredible ripple effect of this?

- Are you getting the sheer power of what you are learning here?

- Do you see how you can be this way any time you choose?

- Do you see how your past need not dictate how you choose to be any longer?

And if you see that this is so, can you see how you have the ability to begin practising to respond in whichever way you choose at any time, and in any place?

Allow yourself to continually feel inspired as you keep writing down everything that being this way makes possible. Also, don't hold back, don't be realistic, have fun with this and let your imagination go. Doing this will enable you to see what your dream entrepreneur lifestyle could be like.

Congratulations for having completed the *7 Point Transformational Mandala System.*

Now let's get you out into the world and being this new way of being which is who you need to be to create and live your dream entrepreneur lifestyle.

STEP 3.

DREAM THE DREAM

"Realism stifles inspiration and inspiration is the very source of the energy required to create spectacular results.

Give up being realistic, let your dreams be grand then commit to find a way to realise them later."

~ Dan Warburton ~

Nothing great is achieved or accomplished without an inspirational end goal, objective or result in mind. However, most people don't ever set *inspirational* or *dream targets*. And even if they think they have, I often find they have set safe, *realistic goals* rather than dream targets that will truly inspire them to take powerful actions every day.

And this is one of the biggest mistakes most professionals and entrepreneurs make.

When a goal is realistic it's usually based on a fear of failing or a fear of the amount of work required to achieve a more ambitious result.

A safe or realistic goal is usually the outcome of being dominated by the survival part of our brain and so it's a goal yet one that is tainted by ensuring you remain safe or ensuring you'll gain approval from others. Therefore, it usually does not come with the level of inspiration required to succeed at achieving something truly inspirational.

You might wish for good health, to be happy or to earn enough money to live – which is absolutely fine. However, such goals are not only too broad and vague but they rarely inspire us enough to take the actions required to live the dream entrepreneur lifestyle.

If you are in a particularly challenging place in your life then go for creating a healthy and happy lifestyle with enough money to live on, as long as this truly inspires you to take the consistent actions to achieve this goal.

That said, these are still likely realistic goals. And even if they inspire you, they likely won't inspire you for long enough to enable you to keep taking the required actions to create any kind of truly fulfilling results.

At a recent event I asked members in the audience, "What is your dream ambition or goal?" The replies were typically: "I want a big house and a new car", "I want to travel" and "I want to be a millionaire."

The problem with these kind of goals (or dreams) is they still rarely awaken enough deep inspiration to enable fulfilling them.

The number one thing that will enable you, the professional, to truly succeed in making your dream lifestyle a reality is a feeling of deep inspiration, and to sustain that inspiration over a long period of time.

Paradoxically this deep inspiration gives a feeling of having arrived already, which makes the journey to achieve such fulfilling results truly wonderful, even before those inspirational goals are tangibly achieved.

I've come to see that the only way to become deeply inspired to achieve such dream goals and feel inspiration for a long period of time is if we virtually live them in our mind on a regular basis. For this reason I take most of my one-to-one coaching clients through my *Dream The Dream* guided meditation exercise.

I enable my client, often a professional or entrepreneur like you who wants to impact the world in a great way, to get comfortable, sit upright in their seat with their eyes open or closed and I then say:

"Imagine that it's three years from today and that you are living your dream lifestyle. That you'd had numerous extraordinary opportunities offered to you, that you then made the most of all those opportunities, that your every proposal was accepted and you completed delivering each service or product extraordinarily well. Imagine that everything had turned out far beyond what you could have ever imagined."

As I get into this process they begin to let go of their daily demands and worries. Then they find themselves moving into a future focused daydream.

This is what this section of the book will enable you to experience.

As you enter into this daydream answer this question:

If you were living your dream entrepreneur lifestyle what would an average day look like for you, from waking up to going to sleep again?

Notice, I ask you what would an *average day* look like for you if you were living your dream entrepreneur lifestyle?

Why? Because such a dream day for you is usually one of a holiday, relaxing with loved ones or one of enjoying a hobby. It's an unsustainable kind of day and the kind of day you wouldn't want to continually experience because soon enough you'd get very bored!

Instead imagine what an *average day* would look like if you were living your dream entrepreneur lifestyle, such as an average day of work in the middle of your week.

As you begin to reflect on this, these questions might help you:

- Where do you wake up?

- Who are you with?

- What is the view like from your window?

- Is it looking over a city, countryside or the sea?

- What is the weather like?

- What is your morning routine?

- What do you do for work?

- How much money are you earning?

- What are you really good at doing?

- Then where do you have lunch?

- Who with?

- Then in the afternoon what do you do?

- Do you continue to work?

- Are you travelling regularly? If so, where to and with whom?

- Maybe in the afternoon you sail a yacht? Or you play golf?

- Maybe you sit under a tree with sea views and read?

- Then for dinner, what do you eat and where? Who with?

- Then what do you do in the evening? Who with?

- What awards do you see on your shelves at home and for what?

- Have you appeared on TV or in a magazine recently for being good at what?

- Whose lives do you elevate and how?

- How many people's lives have you elevated within three years of today?

Then later, as you lie in bed, what are your final thoughts of the day before you sleep?

With the answers to these questions vividly imagined, you can actually feel your dream lifestyle as if you are living it now.

If you do this effectively, momentarily you'll disappear into that daydream. You'll forget where you are now and completely lose yourself in imagining each detail as if you were living that dream lifestyle right now. If you do this effectively, you'll experience wonderful feelings of inspiration rise through you.

This is *Dreaming The Dream*.

The skill is to just dream it. Not to think about making it a reality or to think about *how* it could be created but to simply enjoy letting go and dreaming it so vividly in your imagination that you are left *feeling* as if you really are living your dream lifestyle now. As you experience this allow yourself to *feel* all the feelings of fun and excitement that arise in the process.

This daydream is what I call a *future focused daydream*, which you can re-dream in any moment you choose, and once you have the ability to recall this future focused daydream easily you'll then have a super clear vision or goal to work towards. You will always have a clear indication of what actions are important or not and you will feel the inspiration that's required to enable you to face your inevitable challenges and keep going.

So now, stop everything you're doing and imagine what an average day would look like if you were living your dream lifestyle. If it helps write it down like a series of events that happen from waking up to going to sleep and make sure you include the important areas of your life in this dream such as your family, work, relaxation, health, travel, hobbies, material possessions, finances and anything else you absolutely love or would love to have in your life.

Once you've done this, write down a bullet list of all the elements that existed in your future focused daydream that caused you to *feel* like you were living your dream lifestyle. This list will become your goals and will give you clarity and direction in everything you do. I personally and many of my clients have found this to be extremely effective in enabling us to be in consistent effective action.

A problem you may be faced with is that you are simply not able to stop being realistic because most of the people you spend your time with are predominantly dominated by a realistic or survival-based mindset. So, whenever you voice out loud what inspires you, either none of them listen to you or none of them support you or you are ridiculed and laughed at by them for dreaming such unrealistic scenarios. And so you'll likely give up even before you have started on the quest to fulfilling your dreams.

Because most of your family and friends are likely to be realistic, someone as ambitious as you needs to spend regular time with others who are much more successful than you. Alternatively, you can work with an experienced coach so you can freely voice your dreams to them and participate in an empowering conversation that will enable you to create the solutions you need to make them a reality.

It's highly unlikely that the friends you go drinking with or your work colleagues have the coaching skills required to enable you to create such solutions. I've clearly seen that ambitious people often can't find anyone above their confidence level who can properly support and guide them. Maybe you can relate to this? Do people not understand your ideas and think you're a bit crazy? If so, I know how you feel!

I've been fortunate to have had the courage to invest substantial amounts of my money to work with many amazing coaches but I also make sure that I am continually surrounding myself with people who are much more successful than I am.

In regards to dreaming the dream you must understand that unless the future you choose is an extraordinary one, an unrealistic one, you'll get bored and will soon give up. No one has the ability to stay committed to creating and growing a business if at the end of all the hard work the reward is only to pay rent and bills. I understand that this may be appealing to you right now if you are currently in a financial crisis, but your finances will fall into place once you start being in a way that is required for you to actually realise your dream lifestyle.

Unless you actually play for it, it can never happen.

I once coached a lady in her 40s who was a single mum with two children. For years she'd been a DJ but she no longer enjoyed spending long hours in nightclubs and staying awake until daylight. She wanted to start something different but didn't know what.

During one of our coaching sessions I took her through this *Dream The Dream* process and she saw herself still wanting to uplift people with music at live events but no longer in nightclubs that were frequented by those who consumed a lot of alcohol. She wanted to perform in environments that were vibrant and healthy. After reflecting on our session and attending some networking events she realised that she'd love to organise the music for high-level keynote speakers to enhance their speaking performances while elevating the crowd enjoyment.

Within a few months of receiving coaching from me she became a professional sound engineer for some world-renowned speakers and is now absolutely loving her lifestyle.

I'm not giving you a guarantee that your exact dream lifestyle will become a reality but I can guarantee you that if you implement what I've outlined in this book you will create results that are both extraordinary and beyond what you imagine possible.

To complete this section look back at everything you wrote down to describe what an average day would look like for you if you were living your dream entrepreneur lifestyle. Now write out a bullet list of all the tangible elements that existed in this future focused daydream of yours that made you feel like you were living your dream entrepreneur lifestyle.

This list of tangible elements will then become your list of goals that in the next section I'll show you how to make into your reality.

STEP 4.
CHOOSE THE DREAM –
THE FUTURE FOCUSED
PLAN™

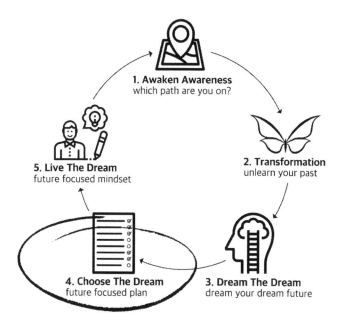

1. Awaken Awareness
which path are you on?

2. Transformation
unlearn your past

3. Dream The Dream
dream your dream future

4. Choose The Dream
future focused plan

5. Live The Dream
future focused mindset

"You'll only reach your destination when you consistently choose it again and again until you arrive."

~ Dan Warburton ~

Once my clients have gone through my *Dream The Dream* guided meditation and written down their dream in a bullet list, I guide them to fill out their *future focused plan.* In this chapter I'm going to also guide you to do the same – the essential step many miss out on the path to tangibly realising their visions.

This section is not to be rushed and I suggest you devote at least four hours to completing this fully. So you might want to spread this section out over a few days. Also enjoy creating this as an artist enjoys making a sculpture. In this case it's you enjoying sculpting your dream lifestyle.

This *future focused plan* is something I've developed over years of intense coaching practice and application. I found that not only do most professionals and entrepreneurs fall into the trap of setting realistic goals but they write a to-do list and think that this is an effective plan. This can start off effectively but before long these lists become a litany of problems to solve and their dream entrepreneur lifestyle soon becomes forgotten. Items on their to-do list soon have little or nothing to do with tangibly living or creating that dream lifestyle.

Because of this tendency I invented *the future focused plan* as a structure designed to enable professionals and entrepreneurs to practise only taking actions that deepen the quality of the present moment while simultaneously creating their dream lifestyle.

To succeed in an extraordinary way you must understand that practising enjoying the journey is crucial because if you don't, when you arrive you won't know you've arrived and you'll likely just continue with the habit of missing your life's precious moments. All you need to do is show up (or be) each day and face challenges in a way that leaves you feeling truly satisfied in yourself.

As the great Brian Tracy states in his book *No Excuses! The Power of Self Discipline:* "Perhaps the most important insight of all with regard to success is that to achieve greatly you must become a different person."

What he means here is that you need to start being the person you need to be to realise all you dream of, if you want to actually realise it. And I've come to see that doing so also leaves us feeling deeply satisfied with ourselves for showing up with such commitment and for taking such courageous action each day.

In this context, the results become secondary and this is the basis of a healthy and happy state of mind. Why? Because as I've said earlier in this book, we can't control anything. We can plan all we like but life will just happen. So if you base your happiness on achieving certain results, you'll become a slave to idealistic desires and you'll waste your life away by always chasing something that today doesn't exist.

This *future focused plan* is designed to enable you to not only enjoy your journey but to ensure you don't continue being in the same way that got you to where you are today, because you now want something new, something greater. Instead this is your plan to ensure you be how you need to be today to create that new and inspirational future. Not only this but being the person you need to be on the journey to your dream lifestyle will leave you feeling fulfilled every day.

As I say to my clients, y*ou must be the future you choose toda*y so this plan is designed to enable you to feel how you will feel when the future you dream of is created, today. However, not just as a *feeling*, as a way of *being* your dream future today. Understanding this is important if you are to create your dream entrepreneur lifestyle.

Once you implement this *future focused plan* you'll soon come to find (as many of my clients have said) that it is extraordinarily effective because it is not problem focused at all, instead it is future focused.

It is also not based on your experiences of your past but is a structure that will enable you to focus on doing what you love or taking important actions to create a lifestyle where you only earn money by doing what you love.

My clients often acknowledge me for having invented this powerful plan.

This plan can be created on an Excel spreadsheet or an online Google sheet so it can be shared with others and accessed from all devices. Maybe you are more familiar with other planning structures so can enter this into another planning program, but be careful to maintain its core layout.

The plan is designed to be filled out from the third milestones first, from three years ahead of today, then section by section back to today.

A simplified version is on the next page.

The Future Focused Plan^{TM}

Area of Life	This week's most powerful actions	1st Milestones (Date)	2nd Milestones (Date)	3rd Milestones (Date)
Being (Now I can be...)				
Health & Wellbeing				
Business				
Finances				
Relationships				
Relaxation & Fun				
Home				
Travel				
Contribution & Legacy				

On the top are the milestones and running down the left are the different areas of your life, which should leave no area of your life not addressed. The reason for including all areas of your life in this is because they are all interconnected. You must gain balance in each area for all of your life to be in balance and deeply satisfying.

There is no point in having great wealth without great health or to have great health without great relationships. In this book you are creating your dream entrepreneur lifestyle, which means wealth and deep fulfilment in every area of your life. So let's get to work.

Regarding the areas of life listed down the left, some of my clients and I find we need to delete, change or add some more categories to suit the dream lifestyle we are each choosing to create.

For instance, the relationship category may not apply to you if you feel totally satisfied with your current relationships. Or you may want to remove the travel section if you are not interested in travelling. Equally you may want to add more areas of life such as business number two, or a hobby or a sport you also want to enjoy practising or excelling at.

With this in mind, check you have every category you need to cover every area of your life. If you are not sure now, you can simply add or remove extra categories as you proceed.

Next, date each milestone.

- The third one is to be dated three years from today

- The second is to be dated two years from today

- The first is to be dated 90 days (12 weeks) from today

I suggest you choose which morning or evening of the week is best for you to complete this. You may prefer a Sunday or Friday evening to plan your actions for the week ahead, it's up to you.

The top area of your life called *Being (now I can be)* is where you enter your new and empowered way of being. It is very powerful to commit to taking on being your new and empowered way of being in every moment you see effective and also as an end goal, as your future focused state to master.

Committing to this means you are committing to practising being this way in every moment you see it to be effective from **now** onwards!

Eventually, this will lose its effectiveness as it will become too familiar, at which point you would need to create a new way of being, but until then begin by filling out the top section of this plan with your empowered state, those three empowering words that you discovered leave you feeling deeply empowered in the top row under the third, under the second, under the first year milestones and as well under this week's actions.

Congratulations, you've now committed to practising being this new way of being from this moment onwards!

Third-Year Milestones

Next, fill in the third-year milestones with the bullet list of the dream elements that you imagined existed as you *dreamed the dream*. Remember how you imagined what an average day would look like if you were living your *dream entrepreneur lifestyle*. You need to fill out each bullet point under each suitable category. Go ahead and do this now to create all your third-year milestones.

Once you've done this you'll likely have other points you realise you want to include such as maybe a health goal or a hobby you'd love to take up, so go ahead and add this now.

By now you should only have the top row filled called *Being* and the right hand column from top to bottom with your third-year milestones.

As you read over your third-year milestones you may start to feel overwhelmed or confronted. If so just catch yourself and come back to being your new and empowered way of being. Also see if rather than think *it'll never happen* or *I lack this* you can maintain a mindset and excitement of *it's coming!*

It's very important to ensure you consistently *feel* empowered.

As you work on your *future focused plan*, don't rush it. I've found that many try rushing through this, which is ineffective. If you are vague on what you choose then you won't be inspired enough to bring these envisioned elements to life. And the actions you'll take will not be focused enough, which will leave you taking scattered actions. If you allow yourself to become clearer and clearer on the dream results you choose to create then every action you'll take will be powerfully aligned to create each specific dream element.

If you do this properly now, you will save a lot of time. Most of my one-to-one clients realise that with their *future focused plan* set up effectively they take fewer actions yet end up creating and achieving so much more than they usually do.

Someone I coached called Sachin who was an online marketing coach couldn't believe how within 90 days after implementing my coaching and his *future focused plan* that he ended up earning more money that he had ever earned before while taking less action than he had taken before.

So, what was it that made this possible for Sachin?

This plan caused him to become totally focused on only taking actions that deepened the quality of his present lifestyle and that also created those exact results he'd dreamed of and chosen. He'd simply de-fluffed his life of the time-wasting actions that no longer served him.

The problem that most encounter when filling out their third milestones is they quickly get lost in negative thoughts such as *This seems totally impossible* or *This is crazy, I'll never succeed at creating all this.* This resigned mindset causes them to overthink, then procrastinate, which leads on to them giving up even before they have started.

Alternatively, many professionals and entrepreneurs (at times myself included) find ourselves needing the third-year milestones to exist immediately to be happy.

We experience a sense of lack in our lives because we have expectations of what we should have achieved by **now** or we compare ourselves to others who have already succeeded in creating beautifully wealthy and balanced lives. Fortunately, I've done this inner work on myself so generally I feel very excited and inspired each day, but most professionals and entrepreneurs live in hope which is a reactionary state of being. It's the opposite of living with inspiration about what could become possible if they maintained being in effective action.

If you are finding yourself experiencing this, you need to find a skilled coach to carry out this deeper work to free yourself of such disempowering ways of being and thinking. You must break free of such disempowered states and embrace a mindset of excitement and fun.

Remember that you will create extraordinary results if you simply keep the inspiration alive in you that your dream entrepreneur lifestyle makes you feel, while using that inspiration to fuel you to take consistent actions that are carefully aligned to actually creating it.

Second-Year Milestones

Now let's get on to your second milestones.

As you look at your third-year milestones, what would need to exist one year before each one for you to be on track to realise each in three years' time?

If it's to have a new business up and running effectively, to own a new dream home or to be an award-winning publisher, then what results would need to be in place a year before each third-year milestone to be on track to achieve them?

Once you can see what needs to exist one year before realising each of the third-year milestones, fill these out under the second milestones.

Well done for getting to this section. I know it can seem laborious but I promise you that once you've done this you'll love how clear and focused you'll feel.

First 90-Day Milestones

Next, complete your first milestones. This is not a year milestone but is actually 90 days (12 weeks) from today. I've come to find that this is just the right length of time ahead to enable us to feel that we can achieve something substantial towards each of the associated second- and third-year milestones, yet the date is close enough to know that we need to get in action right away!

So now go ahead and fill these out.

Each 90-day milestone goal should be enough of a stretch to excite you but not such a stretch that you feel overwhelmed by the thought of it never happening. You are going to need to consistently elevate your state of being as you fill out your *future focused plan* to ensure that the completed version leaves you feeling inspired to keep taking effective action.

Now it's time for you to actually create your dream entrepreneur lifestyle.

Go ahead and fill out each 90-day result you commit to achieving in each category.

This Week's Actions

This section is about you bringing what may seem as unrealistic into reality with powerful action.

Powerful action meaning action that is going to be the very most effective in getting you closer to realising each of your 90-day milestones. These are actions that you commit to carrying out in the next seven days. The art is to choose actions that are small enough for you to actually feel confident to take them but not so big that they leave you feeling overwhelmed and paralysed with procrastination or inaction.

Initial actions might be to call someone you know for advice. Or to hire a new bookkeeper to get your accounts in order. Maybe it's to tell your partner what you are doing and to request their support. Whatever action you know you need to take, just begin by entering it now by each category under the *This Week's Actions* section.

Once you've done this you should be looking at a list of actions that are totally focused on living the life you choose to live *now* while you constructively move towards creating your dream lifestyle of tomorrow. There should be no other actions listed other than actions that enable you to move constructively towards fulfilling your dream results, that enable you be healthy and to enjoy some quality relaxing or fun time. It's this simple.

Can you see how this *future focused plan* is all present and future focused at the same time? Do you see how your past has no place in this? This is what is so powerful about this planning structure.

Finally, for this section you now need to schedule each action in your scheduler.

If your goal is writing a book, making sales calls or some repetitive task then ensure you actually block this time out in your scheduler.

If it's a single action that doesn't require much time then simply block out a time in your scheduler then call this action something like 'refer to *future focused plan*'. Then when you arrive at this time just pick the most important powerful action you've entered first and carry it out in the time you've scheduled.

Whichever way you do this it's up to you, but don't assume you'll get these actions done when you've completed all your other responsibilities. The tasks you feel you have to do or seem as urgent are often a trap. This is you going back to survival mode, being your disempowered interpretation of yourself.

You must actually schedule each action to ensure you have sufficient time or you'll likely never carry out each action and fail to create anything new.

I cannot place enough emphasis on how important actually scheduling your actions into your scheduler is. If you don't do this your life will simply pass you by in a mess of survival.

STEP 5.
LIVE THE DREAM

"Your future will be who you are today."

~ Dan Warburton ~

To *Live The Dream* is both a future-based destination and a way of being in the present moment, simultaneously.

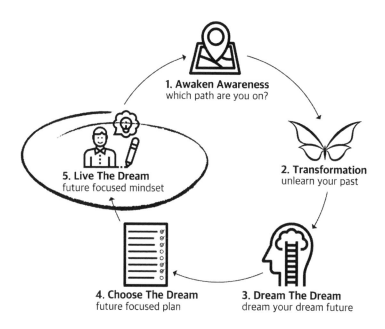

If living the dream was only a future-based destination, we'd be constantly feeling a sense of lack because we'd *feel* like we're not there today.

If to live the dream was purely a present-based intention, we'd all be high and happy but unmotivated to take any consistent actions to create something new and even more fulfilling.

To live the dream is a way of *being*, it is to continually practise taking actions that deepen the quality of the present moment while creating a better future.

In the trilogy *Conversations With God*, author Neale Donald Walsh shares profound insights.

In the first book he wrote: "So do you want your life to *take off*? Begin at once to imagine it the way you want it to be and move into that. Check every thought, word and action that does not fall into harmony with that. Move away from those.

"When you have a thought that is not in alignment with your higher vision, change to a new thought, then and there. When you say a thing that is out of alignment with your greatest idea, make a note not to say something like that again. When you do a thing that is misaligned with your best intention, decide to make that the last time."

Donald (or God if you are open-minded enough!) is saying *be the future you choose to create, now.* In other words, be how you need to be today and ensure that your way of being contains all the actions (and non-actions) required for you to create that dream future that you want to one day realise.

Remember, everything in your life is the way it is now because of how you were being in the past.

I realised this around ten years ago when I had just completed another weekend-long advanced communications course in

London. I gained this huge insight about being and went into absolute shock.

I was frightened by this realisation that I am always responsible for everything I am experiencing in my life in the present moment and therefore also responsible for everything I am going to experience in the future. This was a pivotal realisation for me, that we don't have control over anything but we can choose how we respond. In understanding this at the level of being lies all power to create our dream lifestyle.

Though I've very much come to see that we plan and life happens, we have a choice as to how we be in every moment, even when challenged with adversity. Understanding this is absolutely essential to becoming highly focused and unstoppable.

It took me a few weeks to get my head around this concept because up until this realisation I'd blamed circumstances for why my life was the way it was. This of course was convenient because believing that success was down to luck or subject to circumstances enabled me to avoid taking actions that in truth really scared me.

Instead, I could avoid being focused, I could just pretend to impress others and avoid working effectively. This meant I could avoid producing results that might cause others to find out that *I'm a failure* or that *I'm not good enough, nobody wants me.*

Of course now you and I both know that this was just a disempowering interpretation that I invented about myself. This is why I've written this book for you and laid out this process in the sequence as I have. It was key for you to become aware of what you thought you are not so that you could then allow or create how you choose to be.

First, you had to become honest with yourself about the future you are headed for and you needed to become frightened enough by this grim prospect to want to choose a new and better future.

Then, I took you through my *7 Point Transformational Mandala System* to enable you to become aware of the disempowering ways of viewing yourself that had been running you, that were stopping you feeling empowered and being in action.

During this transformational process I guided you to create yourself in a new and empowered way of being. Once this was done and while in an empowered frame of mind you also created a new space, a new blank canvas on which to *Dream The Dream*. This was where you got to deeply feel the inspirational future that deep down you've always dreamed of living.

Next was the practice of actually choosing it, to plan it out, to break it down into small and easily manageable steps.

Finally, in this section, you are refining being in whichever way you need to be to now be empowered and regularly inspired to take those important weekly actions to actually realise your dream entrepreneur lifestyle.

From now on your mission is to be however you need to be to realise your dreams. To keep checking in with yourself every day, or if you are amidst adversity every minute, to ensure that you are sustaining an effective way of being. You need to do this until this new and empowered way of being becomes natural to you. When you reach this stage you'll no longer need to think about it, you'll just be being it.

From now on I request you choose to play full out. What do I mean by this?

Every day *Dream The Dream*, keep those dreams of yours that truly inspire you alive in you every day, then every day keep asking yourself: Is the action I'm taking now the very most powerful action for me to take to move me towards living my dream entrepreneur lifestyle?

If you find you are not taking the most effective action then stop what you are doing, recalibrate and get back into effective action right away or take a momentary break.

At the same time, always remember that to live the dream is a way of being, it is to continually practise taking actions that both deepen the quality of the present moment while also creating a better future.

Say no to any activity that might be fun in the present moment but damaging to you creating your dream entrepreneur lifestyle. This could be such as spending hours browsing through social media, regularly drinking heavily or registering for another course teaching you a skill that is totally useless. This might be a course in Forex trading which is highly time-consuming when you want to publish a book on the secrets of great parenting.

Equally, also say no to activities that are purely future focused and that are deeply unenjoyable to you. Activities such as studying to gain another PhD when you need to crack how to sell the knowledge you already have, or activities such as working unhealthy long hours purely to get a sales target or promotion. You'll make yourself unwell in the process and in the end your bad health will prevent you enjoying what you already have.

The art is mastering balance in all that you do.

Go forth and be brilliant in the face of everything that life throws at you and when you can't, breathe, rest, reflect then start again.

I want you to understand that there is nowhere to arrive at and there is nothing to chase because the creation of all you dream of is not accomplished by *do-ing* but by *be-ing*, so go forth and be loving, be great and be powerful.

This is to live the *dream entrepreneur lifestyle*. This is to *live the dream, for real*.

FIVE TRUE CASE STUDIES: THE REAL EFFECTS OF TRANSFORMATION

"The only acknowledgment a true leader needs is seeing those he leads succeed."

~ Dan Warburton ~

You may be resigned and disbelieving that what I've covered in this book really is everything you need to do to create and live your dream entrepreneur lifestyle. This is understandable as there are so many different authors, thought leaders and entrepreneurs that state all sorts of opposing approaches to mine to creating such a lifestyle.

Furthermore, you have your own experiences to reflect upon and may have opposing views about what it takes to truly succeed.

There may be many other ideas published and sold as the most effective ways to achieve an extraordinary lifestyle. However most of the professionals and entrepreneurs I've coached through these five steps have uncovered new levels of performance in many areas of their lives and experienced a deeper satisfaction from creating extraordinary results.

Many of the testimonials I've received from the professionals and entrepreneurs I've coached state the extraordinary transformations and results they experienced as a result of my coaching and their implementing of this *5 step reflection transformation system.*

In this section, I will tell you about what my clients achieved from receiving my coaching and from implementing the knowledge I've included in this book.

For more evidence to back up what's covered in this book visit my website and read what my clients say *(www.danwarburton.com)*. Each testimonial comes with a link to their online web spaces so you can ask them about their experiences with the process.

To maintain privacy, I will change names and other details in these case studies. These are recollections of true experiences and events as I can best communicate without disclosing private information.

These inspiring case studies represent the kind of results my coaching clients often experience.

Case Study 1

Name: **James**

Profession: Property Developer

Dream Entrepreneur Lifestyle: **To systemise his property business and become free to travel.**

I was out having some drinks with friends when I met James. He was a highly committed property developer who wanted to create a business that wouldn't need him to micro-manage it. He was doing well financially with ten properties he was renting out. Yet his hands-on business caused him to work from his office at home for long hours each day and on most weekends.

When we began coaching he told me that for over ten years he'd been dreaming of travelling to South America and had always wanted to go to Machu Picchu to see the ancient ruins of the Incas.

The problem was he couldn't ever seem to find a way of freeing himself of his work to travel. He found himself dealing with tenants complaining about noise levels, managing builders to carry out repairs or having to replace tenants whenever they moved out. The demands were never-ending and he just couldn't see a way out of his situation and was resigned to never being able to travel to his dream destinations.

During our second coaching session I took James through my *7 Point Transformational Mandala System.*

He recalled an event when he was seven years old. He remembered travelling with his mother to meet some cousins and other distant family members in Bangladesh for the first time.

They were all sat around a table in a restaurant and James said to his mother, "Mum, I need the toilet." So she replied, "OK darling, follow me." He followed his mother to the back of the restaurant where they ended up in a hallway where local people were waiting. So James asked his mother, "Mum, where is the toilet?" She pointed at some toilet cubicles that didn't have any doors and people were taking their turn, squatting down, with their clothing pulled down to their ankles as they used a hole-in-the-ground-style toilet.

James remembered how scared he felt and how he was thinking there was no way he was going to do the same with everyone watching. As we went deeper in the enquiry he realised that at the time he was thinking *I'm not safe*.

As the coaching conversation went on James quickly realised that this was how he'd interpreted the world and that ever since this event he'd been subconsciously surviving the world as if it really was unsafe. To James the world was dangerous and *not safe*.

James also realised that he'd been trying to control everything in his business out of a fear that if he didn't it would all fall apart and not be financially supportive, and therefore he'd find himself to be in a frightening and unsafe position.

This caused James to try and do everything himself. He feared delegating his business tasks in case others made mistakes and ruined his business. Because of this view of himself and the world, a view that was previously subconscious, he couldn't see any other way. It was just the way the world was for him and he felt that he'd need to work harder and longer hours to succeed.

He was caught in a self-imposed trap. The harder and longer the hours he worked, the less freedom he had, so the harder and longer he thought he needed to work. It was leaving him exhausted and totally resigned.

Then in this coaching conversation with me he had a life-transforming insight.

James realised that he'd *invented I'm not safe*, that it *wasn't true* and he saw that he *no longer needed* to *be* this way. He felt an immense freedom as the weight of having to live in such a world lifted from him.

We continued coaching and in only six weeks after this pivotal coaching conversation he delegated his most time-consuming business activities and bought his ticket to see the Inca ruins at Machu Picchu in South America.

Another six weeks later, James had systemised his business, it was operating without him and he was on a plane to his dream adventure destination. This was something that he wanted to do for over ten years yet couldn't find a way to make it happen. Then in just 12 weeks after these coaching sessions it became a reality.

He sent me photos of himself having the time of his life while seeing the ancient ruins, crossing the Nevada salt flats and meeting other fun-loving travellers. I was so happy for James I was nearly in tears.

I then received a message from James saying that he was going to climb Mount Kilimanjaro in Africa. I couldn't believe it! This man, someone who had been stuck in a little office for years while thinking *I'm not safe*, was now going on adventures and climbing mountains around the world!

He sent me a triumphant photo of him at the top of Africa's highest mountain. I was so excited for him!

On his return he reported that his business had also managed to close a series of larger deals that would double his income within a year.

All of this only became possible for James because he distinguished what disempowering views he had of himself and the world that were holding him back. He then unlearned them, created new ways of being and put structures in place (using his *future focused plan*) to focus his actions to create the dream entrepreneur lifestyle that he'd always wanted.

This realisation for James was so profound that it impacted his life in an extraordinary way. He now enjoys a life with plenty of freedom to travel and he now also gets to play golf every week.

I am still in touch with James and love catching up with him to hear what he's up to while he now gets to live his dream entrepreneur lifestyle.

Case Study 2

Name: **Veronica**

Profession: Yoga Teacher and Fashion Designer

Dream Entrepreneur Lifestyle: **To leave her yoga school and have it run by others so she could find a way of impacting humanity in a deeply fulfilling way.**

Veronica loved practising and teaching yoga. Over five years she had managed to build a successful yoga school. She was leasing a venue on a permanent basis and teaching 12 classes per week. Even though she enjoyed this she didn't feel she was impacting the world in a way that truly inspired her. She wanted to do more but didn't know what or how.

I then took Veronica through my *Dream The Dream* guided exercise and she saw herself as the owner of a highly successful fashion label. Veronica then went on to tell me that she secretly always wanted to have her own fashion label but she never let herself think about actually working towards launching one because she saw it as unrealistic.

Through becoming honest with herself and realising this was her ambition, we began the deeper transformational coaching work with me guiding her through the *7 Point Transformational Mandala System*.

Veronica remembered an event that happened to her when she was eight years old. She was at school and playing in the playground with her classmates. The children decided to play a game of hide and seek and picked Veronica as the one who'd need to find them all. So she covered her eyes with her hands and started counting. The other children played a trick on Veronica and ran back to their classroom.

Once she stopped counting she began searching for her classmates around the playground but the bell rang before she could find them. She went back to her classroom. As she entered they all laughed and pointed at her.

In that moment Veronica remembered feeling excluded and was thinking *I'm not normal, I'm alone.* This caused Veronica to feel that she couldn't ever start a fashion label out of a fear that she might fail and the people she loved might realise she was not normal and exclude her, leaving her alone.

This early experience also meant that Veronica would not express herself fully to others in case they judged her as not normal. Because of this she was very shy and not outspoken. This caused her to not feel heard by others. She wouldn't share her ideas or problems so ironically always felt alone in having to deal with her challenges by herself.

As we went through my *7 Point Transformational Mandala System* she realised that she invented *I'm not normal, I'm alone*, that it wasn't true and she no longer needed to be this way. Like my other clients whom I take through my *7 Point Transformational Mandala System* she experienced a euphoric breakthrough. She felt the weight of such a way of viewing herself lift from her shoulders.

As a result she could clearly see how this way of thinking (and being) had been stopping her from taking actions towards her ambitions and she could now work towards what she really wanted. She saw how this subconscious way of thinking had caused her to play small and maintain a predictable way of living that no longer fulfilled her.

As we then continued coaching over the next few weeks she realised that she wanted to create a revolutionary lifestyle clothing brand. Her clothes were going to be very comfortable for practising yoga yet also so chic that people would want to be seen wearing them out and about. Not only this but the range would be made from totally organic materials, which was somewhat revolutionary in the fashion industry. This would enable Veronica to promote healthy living, inspire others to be caring towards our environment, and in the process show others how it's possible to become financially successful in a truly caring way.

Within four weeks of her initial breakthrough she came up with the brand name as well as employing a designer and a tailor to bring her ideas to life. In just 12 weeks after starting coaching with me she'd made the prototypes, had a full collection of yoga pants made and was travelling around Europe attending yoga events and giving live demonstrations from the stage about her fashion label. Veronica had become a totally transformed lady and her results proved this.

Soon she had her tailor working round the clock to keep creating new yoga pants to sell. Her idea had taken off.

As we continued coaching I reminded her of her old limiting way of thinking so that she could day by day, moment by moment, be who she chooses to be. This gave Veronica the ability of being how she needed to be to succeed in creating and launching her dream fashion brand.

Veronica quickly proved that her yoga pants sold, that there was a market for her designs and so she went on to create a business plan. I spoke to her recently and she said how she's now found suppliers of organic fabric that she loves that can cope with larger demand and she's found factories in Portugal that are ready to produce her clothes in larger volumes.

She is now in the final stages of negotiations with a major investor in the UK who is set to grant Veronica the capital she requires to launch her brand across all of Europe.

One year later since we began coaching she is still totally lit up with inspiration, is teaching fewer of her yoga classes and is now loving her journey as the leader of a revolutionary fashion brand.

Veronica is now living her dream entrepreneur lifestyle.

Case Study 3

Name: **Sandra**

Profession: Nutritionist

Dream Entrepreneur Lifestyle: **To attract high-paying one-to-one clients and afford to freely travel to exotic places around the world.**

Sandra was a person who used to find social events very awkward. She found it difficult to introduce herself or express her ideas clearly. When we began working together Sandra was working in a company that offered nutritional guidance to people running in marathons. Her role was to hold one-to-one meetings with the runners to help them make the best choices regarding their diet. Her objective was to ensure that their diet enabled them to run effectively while being nutritionally balanced.

Her problem was that she wasn't being paid much in her employed position. And she kept finding herself either totally burned out with the demands of her employers, or when the marathon season was over she'd find herself out of work and not earning enough to live off during these low periods.

I initially guided her through the *Awaken Awareness* process.

Sandra realised that she was headed for a future she really did not want. She could see she was doomed to settling for an unfulfilling employment position. She had to do something differently but didn't know what or how she could get herself out of her repetitive employment situation.

Sandra also yearned to be recognised for her skills as a nutritionist but didn't feel valued by her employer for all her hard work. She was feeling frustrated with the intermittent marathon seasons which caused her to go through boom and bust cycles. What she really wanted was to be able to earn good money consistently from self-employment and have the freedom to travel to exotic places.

During the *7 Point Transformational Mandala System* she remembered an event that happened when she was seven years of age. She remembered sitting on her bed at home with her sister in her room and hearing their parents arguing and shouting in the kitchen downstairs. She remembered hearing a plate being smashed against a wall. She then heard the front door being opened and slammed shut. After this everything went quiet.

So she slid off her bed and ran to look out of her bedroom window and she saw her father quickly walk across the front garden, open the metal gate then disappear as he walked away.

She thought her father had left the family because of her, because she was *not important, I'm not needed.*

During the coaching conversation Sandra realised she'd interpreted herself as *I'm not important, I'm not needed.* Deeper into the transformational enquiry I coached her to look at the unwanted impacts of her being this way in her life. She was shocked.

Sandra realised that everything she had done ever since that moment when her father walked out of their house was to ensure that nobody would ever find out that she wasn't important. She could see why she created all the unfulfilling experiences and struggles trying to earn money doing what she loved.

Sandra realised how she always said yes to requests by her bosses. This caused her to work long hours, settle for a low wage and feel she was always being bullied into doing unrewarding tasks. She feared saying no as this would cause her to lose her job, fail and be discovered as *not important.*

Sandra also realised how this affected her ability to introduce herself effectively. She would go to networking events (that's how I met her) but she would find it difficult to speak about what she does with authority and passion. She would rarely effectively promote herself for all her knowledge of nutrition.

This pattern of hers came from a fear she had that people might judge her and consider her as unimportant. The outcome was no one would hire her for her nutritionist skills because her manner communicated a lack of confidence in what she did, so this caused people to not trust her abilities. This vicious cycle caused her to experience a lack of results that reinforced this disempowering view of herself which was that she really wasn't important. This was a life-changing realisation for Sandra.

As with my other clients she became aware that she'd invented such a disempowering interpretation, that it wasn't true and that in her case she no longer needed to be *I'm not important, I'm not needed.*

Sandra finally set herself free of this crippling way of viewing herself and the world.

Because she was no longer dominated by this she was able to start effectively pitching what she does to others. She started introducing herself to everyone she met as a nutritionist who specialises in enabling people to heal from diabetes and hormone imbalances. Within only four weeks she had attracted her first high-paying client.

Over the 12-week period that I coached Sandra she managed to resign from her job that she's been in for years and her business took off. She created a series of high-paying clients and booked her flight to Burma. She also started to collaborate with some highly recognised diabetes specialists in the UK about teaming up with them to put on a major live event to promote diabetes awareness.

Sandra's outlook totally transformed and so did her life. She shared pictures on Facebook of her having a great time with a friend in Burma and more recently photos of her relaxing on a beach and drinking wine with friends at a prestigious resort in the south of France. It's evident that she has continued to succeed and is now living her dream entrepreneur lifestyle.

Nothing fulfills me more than seeing entrepreneurs succeed and enjoy life.

Case Study 4

Name: **Wendy**

Profession: Freelance Business Lawyer

Dream Entrepreneur Lifestyle: **To leave her freelance business she'd had for over 12 years, and start a new inspiring creative business.**

When Wendy approached me for help she was exhausted and depressed. Wendy was in her 50s, struggling to lose weight and wanted to implement a better health routine. She also more than anything wanted to break out of her current working situation and had wanted to do so for over 12 years. In her work she had to deal with endless incoming piles of heavy paperwork so she rarely had time to relax, enjoy life or properly take care of her wellbeing.

She found the business law industry to be dominated by people who wanted to follow outdated protocol. This meant that people in disputes over employment laws or business deals would usually be guided through the lengthy process of going to court. This was often financially damaging for one or both parties and Wendy saw that it rarely left the people involved with a satisfying outcome. She disliked this system and wanted to offer people an alternative solution to court.

During my *7 Point Transformational Mandala System*, Wendy also broke free from her disempowering, past-event based way of viewing herself and the world, which was *I'm not good enough, I'm not clever enough*. In becoming free of this limiting way of viewing herself she was able to reinvent herself and become clear about her services.

In the *Dream The Dream* process she visualised a new future not only for herself but for the whole of the employment and business law sector. She had the insight to create a completely new way to serve people who were amidst business and employment disputes. She saw that rather than defending clients in court, she could offer a mediation service. She wanted all parties in disagreements to avoid the stressful courtroom conflict and instead settle disputes in a more humane way.

Once Wendy realised this, she was standing in front of an inspiring new future and felt an excitement that she hadn't felt for years!

In filling out the third-year milestones of her *future focused plan,* she could clearly visualise her dream future. She then broke down the big picture into tiny, manageable weekly actions.

She declined contracts that demanded her to operate in the usual ways the law industry expected. Instead, she began offering her new mediation services.

It was challenging to turn down lucrative work but each week on her video call with me we refined her message and actions. Within six weeks she had rebranded herself and updated her website to offer her new services.

She also tackled her health issues by including health targets in her *future focused plan.* She stopped drinking a glass of wine every evening, she hired a personal trainer and started attending gym three times a week. Initially, getting fit wasn't easy but with the encouragement of our transformational coaching sessions each week she mastered a new routine.

The quality of her lifestyle soon elevated to new heights. She was able to achieve all this because she was no longer surviving old ways of viewing the world while simultaneously creating her new dream future. Wendy felt inspired again and woke each day feeling excited about who she might have the opportunity to serve.

By the end of a six-month one-to-one coaching course with me Wendy had attracted many new clients who received her mediation services while she chose to keep some clients that she defended in the traditional manner through the court system.

Wendy was feeling healthy and energetic again and as though she was genuinely living her purpose. She was elated as she told me how her life had transformed and I could see she really was now living her dream entrepreneur lifestyle.

Case Study 5

Name: **Mandy**

Profession: Chief Marketing Officer for an Expo Events Company

Dream Entrepreneur Lifestyle: **To restructure the dynamics in her current employment position so she can work the hours she chooses with flexibility to become a property investor.**

Mandy wrote to me after she'd heard about the results my clients were achieving from receiving my coaching. So we set up an initial call. Mandy opened up to me about how she was feeling totally burned out, stressed, with no time to create and live the lifestyle she yearned for.

She was earning a fairly good monthly wage but was often on call on a 24-hour basis. She'd often travelled to other countries to lead teams to create effective marketing and advertising campaigns for expo events. With the different time zones, she was working very long hours to cover all these projects. The work was leaving her feeling totally exhausted and the travelling disrupted her routine so she could not maintain a daily fitness regime.

In coaching Mandy realised she wasn't setting boundaries for how she wished to be treated in her employment position. She let her CEO and other team leaders manipulate her into taking on roles she had not agreed to in her original employment contract. This pressure caused Mandy to be defensive and angry. She'd get frustrated that people didn't listen to her and follow her requests. She believed she had to take over other people's work to ensure each country's team got the expected results.

We found a whole series of views about herself that caused the deeply unfulfilling employment dynamics she was experiencing. The subconscious views dominating her were *I'm trapped, I have no choice, I'm not important. I'm not loved* and *I'm powerless, I'm not enough.*

She invented these views during events that happened before she was 13 when she was in circumstances where she felt frightened and embarrassed.

For Mandy, though these events were not traumatising, they were still challenging enough to cause her to invent such disempowering views of herself. This meant she had to constantly defend herself by shouting and being short-tempered with others. When she felt she couldn't control a colleague above her in authority she would agree to any chore just to please them.

It was these ways of being that Mandy took on to ensure she wouldn't be trapped, that she'd have choice, that she'd be seen as important, loved and as if she really was good enough. The problem was that in being this way this caused her to experience the very opposite: she'd lost her freedom in her work and lost her ability to be fully self-expressed.

During our coaching conversations she awoke to see she'd invented all this, that none of it was true and that it was only her who thought these things of herself. She was then able to set herself free of being dominated by such crippling ways of thinking. Soon Mandy was able to say no to requests not agreed in her contract and she learned to make calm but powerful requests of her team leaders.

Next, I taught her how to inspire others to take effective action. Because of her calm and caring tone, her team leaders started to listen to what she had to say. Within six weeks of coaching, the departments she led achieved significant increases in their performance.

She since requested a new contract where she'd work less, only have the roles she enjoyed and still earn the same salary. She was able to close a new employment contract that made her happy.

Mandy now travels less frequently, has found a whole new level of enjoyment in her job, has plenty of time off to enjoy activities she wants to do, has a great daily fitness routine and is successfully investing in various other projects that she now loves working on.

Mandy is now living her dream entrepreneur lifestyle.

These are five case studies based on my clients' achievements that I've randomly chosen to tell you about to demonstrate how powerful the knowledge is in this book. However, I've had many of my other clients achieve further extraordinary results.

One is a health and fitness instructor who doubled his income through creating new one-on-one clients and generated over $45,000 in less than a month.

Another had been trying to sell her accountancy company for over seven years then, while in one of my one-on-one programmes, she sold her business for $400,000 and another went from being an unknown project manager to creating A-list celebrity clients under her own brand, some of which included members of the British Royal Family.

These clients of mine achieved such results because they implemented what I've covered in this book.

So, don't let this just be more information you've taken in, actually implement what I've taught you and watch what happens.

YOUR LIFE AFTER THIS BOOK

"Those who don't accomplish much wait for their fear to disappear. Those who accomplish great things surrender to knowing they'll always feel it."

~ Dan Warburton ~

To now ensure your greatest possible success you need to live the dream as a way of being. This means to continually take actions that both deepen the quality of the present moment while creating a better future.

So what does this look like on an ongoing and practical basis?

Each week you need to review your *future focused plan*. That's a weekly commitment.

First and foremost, tick all the things you have accomplished and celebrate them.

Stop for at least 15 seconds to see all the things you've accomplished and allow yourself to feel good about everything you've accomplished, however small each task. Accept that even sitting down to check if you are on track or not warrants you to be rewarded as this in itself is a powerful action that most entrepreneurs avoid.

Acknowledging yourself for having completed the actions you've set will make it easier for you to feel inspired and easier to continue being how you need to be to create your dream future.

If you make a commitment to always acknowledge the small actions you complete you'll find that doing so will build and build momentum for you in an extraordinary way.

Each week read over the third-year milestones of the dream future you are choosing to live. Allow yourself to not feel you lack those things but that they are coming. Allow yourself to feel excited as you *Dream The Dream* and imagine living your life like this.

If you find goals in your third-year milestones are stereotypical goals you've set simply because you believe you should be like everyone else, then delete them. Let them go. Not everybody wants a mansion in Beverly Hills! To some this location might be too congested and noisy and a mansion far too big to worry about having to maintain and keep clean!

Maybe you've chosen to have a company with 12 centres around the world but, what if you could find a way of making just one centre produce adequate profit to experience everything you wish for while requiring a lot less work?

Usually more does not equal happy so review your third-year milestones at least every three months and keep fine-tuning your dream destination.

Alternatively, you might have other things you've realised you'd love to have in your life such as being able to play a musical instrument, supporting children in orphanages or buying an old chateau in the South of France to renovate.

Whatever your dream is, write it down in your *future focused plan*, then in reverse create your milestones towards the vision, right down to this week's tiny, tiny actions.

There are all sorts of planning structures out there and I tried implementing many of them but none I've found to be as simple or effective as this one.

I found many other planning structures were too complicated. Whenever something didn't go to plan or happen on time I'd have to re-plan all over again and change all intermediary goals to be back on track. It meant I spent so much time planning rather than being in action. Some people enjoy planning and we also know that good planning can enable us to need to take fewer actions to achieve our desired results, so do what works for you.

This *future focused plan* is the simplest and fastest way I know of planning all the important actions we need to take to create and live our dream lifestyle.

Each week, once you've read over your third-year milestones, refine them (if need be), then after you've felt a little of that inspiration again, update the second milestones.

I suggest you do not compromise on the 90-day milestones unless you genuinely find something more inspiring you'd love to commit to achieve. But be careful that you are not simply changing the 90-day milestones to avoid taking the necessary actions that are required for you to truly succeed!

Ideally these 90-day milestones should only be updated when the 90-day mark has passed. Only then would you erase them and set new ones that are again totally aligned with your third and second milestones.

Then each week, re-plan the coming week's most powerful actions you see to take. Delete the actions you have taken and leave the ones you haven't. There is no effectiveness whatsoever in getting angry with yourself or blaming yourself for not taking the remaining actions. Do not do this. Instead simply acknowledge what you didn't do with no judgment laid upon yourself. Then get back to feeling inspired about the actions you can take going forward. The more you practise this, the better you'll get at this habit that will make you absolutely unstoppable at just getting back in action each week.

A great ratio of weekly actions to complete is eight out of ten. If it's less than this then maybe you're setting the bar too high each week, which will cause you to not complete all the actions you've committed to. This could leave you feeling less rewarded.

Alternatively, if you complete ten out of ten actions each week you could feel more rewarded, however you'll likely be playing small and thus wouldn't be growing in your abilities as effectively as you could be.

It's up to you to choose the actions to take each week. Just ensure that the ones you choose you know for sure you can complete but actions that also leave you feeling a little stretched. Get this balance right and you'll wake up every day feeling totally alive.

Before filling out each of your weekly actions keep in mind what we've covered in the previous paragraphs, then ask yourself:

What are the most important actions for me to take to realise my dream lifestyle?

As you begin seeing the most important actions to take, add them to this week's actions. Move these to your scheduler and actually block in the times you'll carry out each action.

Keep updating and implementing your *future focused plan* every week!

While doing this and during your weeks ahead continually practise being your new and empowered way of being moment by moment. You are going to need to be this even when things don't go to plan for you to be on track.

Finally, continually feel the inspiration of knowing that if you keep being empowered your dream entrepreneur lifestyle is coming to you, for real!

I've now coached over 1,000 individuals to implement the exact steps I've covered in this book and many have now gone on to successfully create extraordinarily fulfilling lifestyles for themselves. Admittedly they achieved such results because they received consistent coaching from me – so I know you'll likely not implement what I've outlined in this book effectively. Why? Because you are simply in the way of yourself!

Maybe you are still procrastinating and avoiding doing what you know you need to do.

Maybe you feel stuck in a job you don't enjoy, you are recovering from a break-up, your business is failing or you are simply resigned or depressed. Maybe you are in an overwhelming situation where you have so much going on that you can't focus, or maybe you are simply unclear on the way to move forward.

Do any of these experiences resonate with you?

If you find yourself experiencing any of these blocks, feel stuck in some way or are facing challenges and want to break through so you can create a completely new and inspirational future then go to:

www.danwarburton.com

There I have free resources to help you gain the insights and knowledge you need.

Your future is now powerfully in your own hands.

Whatever you do, remember dream the dream, choose the dream, live the dream!

References

Hill, N. (1937, 2012). *Think and Grow Rich.* Qingdao Publishing Group.

Lakhiani, V. (2016). *The Code of the Extraordinary Mind.* Rodale Books.

Litvin, R. & Chandler, C. (2013). *The Prosperous Coach.* Maurice Bassett.

Singer, M.A. (2015). *The Surrender Experiment.* Harmony Publishers.

Sharma, R. (1996). *The Monk Who Sold His Ferrari.* HarperCollins Publishing.

Tracy, B. (2010). *No Excuses! The Power of Self Discipline.* Vanguard Press.

Walsch, N.D. (1996). *Conversations With God.* Berkley Publishing.

Walsch, N.D. (1997). *Conversations With God.* Hodder & Stoughton.

Yogananda, P. (2010). *The Law Of Success.* Snowball Publishing.

Appendix

Step 2: 7 Point Transformation Mandala System Activities

1. Occurrence

Be honest with yourself and write down how these circumstances cause you to truly *feel.*

Which area of your life isn't the way you would prefer or choose it to be, right now?

What if nothing changed? How do I feel about this area of my life always being the same as it is now?

Ask:

- How do I feel when things don't go to plan or take much longer than planned?

- How do I feel when someone is late for a meeting and doesn't communicate?

- How do I feel when I'm not paid on time or when I don't have enough money?

2. Physiology

Ask:

- Where in my body do I feel the feelings I wrote down?

- And what is that feeling like?

3. Recalling

Ask:

- When was the first time I ever felt these physical feelings?

Record your recollections.

4. Interpretation

Ask:

- What was I thinking at the time, starting with *I am... or I am not...*

Write what comes to you that is most predominant.

5. Breakthrough

- What are the unwanted impacts that I have in my life as a result of me being (insert your disempowering interpretation here)?

Examples:

- What are the unwanted impacts that I have in my life as a result of me being (*I'm not good enough, nobody wants me*)?

- What are the unwanted impacts that I have in my life as a result of me being (*I'm not clever, I'm small*)?

Write your list

Part B

Ask:

- What will my life look like in one year if I continued to be this way?

Part C

Ask:

- Do I get how destructive this way of being is for me and my life?

- Do I see how this way of being will cause me to never be able to succeed to the level I could?

- Do I see how this way of being does not serve me any longer?

- Who invented this way of being? Really? (I invented this)

- Is this way of being true?

- Do I need to be this way any longer?

6. Empowered State

Ask:

- Now that I no longer need to be (enter here your disempowering interpretation), I can be (enter here some words that leave you feeling empowered)

List three words that describe an empowered state that inspires you.

7. Full Expression

- If I chose to be (enter your three most empowering ways of being here) what would become possible for me, and my life?

- ... and what does that make possible? For example:

- If you chose to be this way in your next meeting what could the outcome be?

- If you chose to be this way on stage to showcase who you

are and what you do and pitch a service or a product what could become possible?

- If you chose to be this way with the people you love, with your neighbours, colleagues at work and with everyone new you met what could become possible?

- If you chose to be this way in the face of your every challenge and situation you are to face what could become possible?

List responses.

About the Author

Dan Warburton, a well-travelled British entrepreneur, is someone who has always had a great ambition to create, live and share an extraordinary lifestyle yet he spent a major part of his life dealing with sadness, anxiety and frustration.

The cause of his deep dissatisfaction was a feeling of not fitting in at school, failing to succeed in numerous business ventures and not being able to make his father proud. From his mid-20s and throughout his 30s Dan became determined to discover why he found himself continually failing to create even one single satisfying business and so he turned to self-development and deep reflection for the answer.

Dan read hundreds of books about leadership and success in an attempt to find that missing key to breaking through to the next level. He implemented what he learned from reading many books such as *The Monk Who Sold His Ferrari* by Robin Sharma, *Think and Grow Rich* by Napoleon Hill, *Losing My Virginity* by Sir Richard Branson, *A New Earth* by Ekhart Tolle, *The 4 Hour Work Week* by

Timothy Ferris and *The Richest Man in Babylon* by George Clason.

Along with his constant yearning for knowledge from great authors, Dan also spent time learning to meditate with Buddhist monks, he practised Tai Chi for years and was awarded a Tai Chi Master certificate and practised yoga under great teachers in India and in the Himalayas.

All of this was to enhance his abilities in creating and living the greatest lifestyle a human possibly can.

In the end Dan attended over 200 courses in self-development that covered ontology (the study of being), leadership and self-transformation, which is now his primary focus.

With his envious lifestyle and numerous testimonials online from entrepreneurs stating that his coaching dramatically elevated the quality of their lifestyle, Dan is now seen as the pioneer of transformational coaching and is invited to speak at events around the world about what transformation makes possible for those who truly want to succeed.

What makes Dan happier than anything is coaching professionals and entrepreneurs, seeing them impact humanity in a great way and in the process create and live their dream lifestyle.

From his own journey and from having coached over 1,000 entrepreneurs, Dan Warburton reveals in this book his greatest insights about what it takes to succeed in an extraordinary way as an entrepreneur.

Contact Me

If at any stage of reading this book you'd like to contact me with your thoughts or ideas, if you'd like me to speak at an event, or if you are interested in collaborating in some way then you'll find details to contact me at:

www.danwarburton.com

Apply For A Complimentary Coaching Call

If you are interested to find out more about how to receive one-on-one coaching from me or would like to apply for a complimentary strategy and insights coaching session with me then go to www.danwarburton.com for more details.

I'll then reply with a link for you to apply for this.

Your future is now powerfully in your own hands.

A Letter from Dan to You

Hi

Thank you very much for reading this book and for giving me the opportunity to serve you.

If you have an ambitious friend who isn't in a good place right now or who you think would gain useful insights from reading this book, then please send them a copy as a gift. They'll be touched by your kind gesture. You can do so by going to:

dreamorder.danwarburton.com

If you'd like to buy discounted bulk orders of this book for your friends, colleagues or to give to future event attendees then email us at:

service@danwarburton.com

Bulk orders over a certain number come with me attending an event for you as a speaker or trainer at no extra charge.

If you'd like to be part of my private Facebook group where I share exclusive content about transformation for entrepreneurs and insights in how to become a highly profitable expert then go to:

exclusivegroup.danwarburton.com

Please leave a review of this book for me on Amazon. This will cause awareness of the book to spread so together we'll impact more lives, this would mean so much to me.

Whatever you do, dream the dream, choose the dream, live the dream.

All the very best

Dan Warburton

Printed in Great Britain
by Amazon